ACCLAIM FOR

Lito Tejada-Flores's
BREAKTHROUGH ON SKIS

"Tejada-Flores has one of the brightest, most unconventional minds in ski teaching today. His approach is as entertaining as it is instructive."
　　—Dick Needham, editor in chief, *Ski* magazine

"Tejada-Flores breathes fresh wind into the sails of intermediates and advanced skiers alike who feel trapped in the doldrums. The most practical and world-wise book on advanced skiing to appear in the last 20 years." 　　　　　　　—*Snow Country* magazine

"Lito is unmatched in his ability to see through complex technical gobbledygook, to explain concepts clearly and simply. He's written a wonderful introduction to expert-level skiing, one that will be useful not only to intermediate skiers but even to veteran instructors looking for fresh, effective ways to teach."
　　—Seth Masia, technical editor, *Ski* magazine and author of *Ski Magazine's Managing the Mountain*

"Written by a discerning ski teacher who knows how to sequence information without reducing it to a thin linear trail, the book engages the senses in such a way that images leap to the mind's interior screen."
　　—Denise McCluggage, author of *The Centered Skier,* writing in *Snow Country* magazine

BREAKTHROUGH ON SKIS

How to Get Out of the Intermediate Rut

by Lito Tejada-Flores

VINTAGE BOOKS
A DIVISION OF
RANDOM HOUSE, INC.
NEW YORK

to my students who always taught me as much as I taught them, and who eventually convinced me there really was an expert in every skier

ACKNOWLEDGMENTS

I'd like to thank a number of good friends who helped me with this book: Pete Feistman of the Vail Ski School, Bill Grout of *Skiing Magazine* and Neil Stebbins of *Powder Magazine,* for their support and their devilishly perceptive comments; Bob Craig of the Keystone Center for taking the manuscript under his wing and successfully pushing it out of the nest into the real world; and most of all, Linde Waidhofer, the most sensitive ski teacher I know, as well as my true love, for reading the manuscript over and over and always telling me honestly which parts needed rewriting.

INTRODUCTION TO THE 1993 EDITION

Hype or Hope: Is There an Expert In Every Skier?

The first edition of *Breakthrough on Skis* was a kind of crazy dare, a bet against uncertain odds, a long shot. Against all conventional wisdom, I claimed that most skiers—virtually *all* skiers—could ski like experts, and that the only reason they didn't was that they just didn't know how expert skiers did it. I also claimed that expert skiing was not simply an improved, polished version of intermediate skiing. It was something else; not harder, just different. And I set out to prove there was an expert in every skier with this collection of techniques and tactics—which are all you need to break out of the intermediate rut to a higher level of skiing performance.

It worked. I won the bet, and so did the more than 65,000 skiers who have bought and read *Breakthrough on Skis,* and as a result totally changed their way of skiing. So why a new edition now? Has skiing changed that much? Is expert skiing today, and the path that will get you there, any different? You'll be glad to know it isn't. What worked five years ago works today. Real expert skiing has been called "classic skiing." It's functional, not faddish.

This point was brought home more clearly than ever last winter while I was filming the video version of *Breakthrough on Skis*. I had the pleasure of filming and skiing and talking with some of the finest skiers in the country, from Olympic medalists to national demo-team members. I had watched these same skiers perform for years, and the video images only underlined the continuity of their style. Real expert technique is nothing more than the personal application of a few, a very few basic technical elements. The movement patterns of expert skiing have changed only slightly and subtly in a decade or so—the key breakthrough elements described in chapters two, three and four of this book are still so up-to-date that I was able to build *Breakthrough on Skis: The Video* around them.

Indeed, developments in ski equipment occur much more quickly than changes in technique. And that's where most of the new material in this edition comes from. Exciting innovations in ski design continue to make high-level skiing easier year after year. In particular, skis for powder snow have come a long way since I wrote *Breakthrough on Skis*—a real revolution in the deep. So it seemed high time to revise a couple of chapters.

But let's go back to the beginning. I'd like to tell you why so few skiers ever become real experts, and just what we can do about it. . . . Skiing is no longer hard. Anyone, nowadays, can become a sloppy, rough-and-ready, parallel (or "parallelish") skier in a couple of weeks, a couple of weekends. The initial freedom such skiers enjoy is fabulous. Soon they can ski down almost every run on the mountain. They learn to cope with—and to survive—a pretty high degree of difficulty. And then . . . ?

There's the rub. Most skiers stop improving somewhere in the intermediate, or advanced-intermediate, range. They can get down almost anything. But on tough slopes this means survival skiing, just hanging on—certainly not dancing down, light, deft, effortless, the way real experts do. Worse yet, there's no obvious way to make that quantum leap to expert skiing. Typically, advanced ski-school classes, even private lessons, give you lots of intriguing tips, but they don't really change the way you ski.

So what's wrong? Why do the majority of skiers fall into this trap, the intermediate doldrums? Why is the average skier with five to ten years of experience still not an expert, but only a plateaued-out, slightly frustrated intermediate, aware that there's another, higher level of skiing, but with no idea how to reach it? My explanation hangs on several factors. Part of the blame has to be laid on the very successful, accelerated way we teach beginners these days. We have traded long-term options for short-term success by stressing a wide, equally weighted stance and simple two-legged steering movements that produce instant results, but that also become a kind of security blanket, a crutch, that keeps our students from developing a repertoire of advanced skills and advanced balance.

Second, a comendable but ultimately confused focus on ski-teaching psychology has been largely counterproductive. American ski teachers have embraced the idea of "Inner skiing," and a host of other holistic and "head-trip" approaches to teaching, often mistakenly substituting them for technique. The point is, head trips alone won't cut it. You can't talk, con, or even hypnotize yourself into feeling like an expert skier if your legs and feet don't possess expert skills to control your skis.

And finally, the time factor. A first-day beginner can learn a hell of a lot in one hour. A novice can totally transform his or her way of skiing in one day with a good instructor. But an advanced-intermediate can't hope to achieve any lasting change in one lesson, or in one day. I would say that a week—five days of concentrated effort, anyway—is the minimum time span for a plateaued, upper-level skier to make a real breakthrough. Yet typically when a ski school offers a special program or workshop for advanced skiers, it's even shorter than a regular lesson. The assumption—which I believe is false—is that good skiers are far too impatient to concentrate on their skiing for a longer period. Naturally, this approach doesn't work. No wonder the upper levels of our ski schools are relatively deserted compared to the full beginner and novice classes. But it doesn't have to be this way.

How do I know? Let me share with you the most exciting, most rewarding ski teaching experience I've ever had—the experience that grew into this book. Some years ago, working as technical director of the Squaw Valley Ski School in Lake Tahoe, I finally said, "Enough! It's time to find out whether it's possible to turn average skiers into super-skiers." So I organized a program we called *The Ski Clinic at Squaw.* It was a total-saturation, five-day ski course, designed expressly for frustrated upper intermediates (parallel skiers or better). And it worked like a charm! These were the most motivated students I'd ever skied with. We skied in small groups. We videotaped the skiers every day, and we finished the week by comparing a tape of our skiers arriving on Monday with their final performance on Friday, which showed a mind-boggling difference. Above all, we managed to run a very technical, very "outer skiing," week-long workshop that wasn't at all boring but was, in fact, highly adventurous and challenging. We promised—and delivered—major breakthroughs; we actually produced expert skiers.

But such intense teaching/learning situations are rare indeed. They are difficult, complex, and expensive to organize and run. For a number of reasons, including lack of imagination, most ski areas and ski schools aren't even willing to consider such programs. Business as usual is so much easier.

This book contains in written form what we offered so successfully at Squaw Valley. A no-nonsense, achievable promise of a major breakthrough on skis. Of course, I'd rather ski with you for a week. But I think we can work the same magic together with this book.

I should warn you that when I talk about the secrets of expert skiing, I'm not really talking about short cuts; no one becomes an instant expert. You will still have to pay your dues, practice a lot, struggle a little, build your success turn after turn, run after run, day after day. In only one sense does this book offer a kind of short cut. I'm offering you a *simplified* program, the shortest path I know to get there. I stress the absolute minimum number of techniques and technical elements—not the full gamut of all possible techniques, only the key *common denominators* found throughout expert skiing. There are fewer of these indispensable basics than one would imagine. But their combinations, recombinations, and applications to an ever-changing world of snow and steepness are almost infinite.

I can't condense the secrets of a whole sport into just a few sentences. But I can tell you, as a kind of preview, that the main thrust of your progress toward expert skiing will entail getting progressively more and more performance from your equipment while supplying less and less physical force with your own muscles. It's a nice surprise to realize that expert skiers are, in their own way, a little lazy. Or is that just a sign of efficiency?

I encourage you to read the next section, "Strategy: How to Use This Book," before tackling the text. Skiers of different levels should begin at different points. As a matter of fact, we'll all end at different points, too. For expert skiing is wide open, a world of possibilities, not just one rigid style of skiing. My definition of an expert is someone who is completely at home on his or her skis. Equally at home on any slope, in any snow, at any speed, making—or better, playing with—any size, shape, or style of turn. Sound good? I thought so.

Lito Tejada-Flores
August 1993

CONTENTS

STRATEGY

How to Use This Book

Throughout this book I'm going to talk to you as simply and directly as I talk to my ski students, or friends, on the hill. But just who are *you?* It's true, I have a sort of typical reader in mind, but I know that *you* come in all shapes and sizes, with different skiing backgrounds and aspirations. So it's time to do a little sorting out and steer you toward the parts of the book that will do you the most good.

In general, I've written this book for skiers who've been at it for some time, who aren't really satisfied with the way they ski, and—most important—who want to do something about it. Frustrated skiers, if you will, but ambitious skiers—not timid ones. This partly explains the lack of head-trip advice on how to psych yourself up to a better performance, or how to un-psych yourself out of a nervous frame of mind. But my bias toward technical solutions runs deeper. Most mental/emotional hangups on skis are a direct result of not being able to cope physically—and that means technically—with conditions on the mountain. It's more helpful to show a panic-stricken beginner how to slow down and stop, than to try to talk him out of his fear. That's more or less what I plan to do with all of you who want to become expert skiers: share the technical secrets that really matter and let you build your own confidence on a real, not an imaginary foundation.

If you fit into my target readership—with at least a couple of years of serious if not spectacular skiing under your belt—you may want to skip chapter one ("Basics") and turn directly to the next three chapters. These three chapters (two, three and four) form the centerpiece of this book. They concentrate on and reveal what I believe are the minimum critical skills of expert skiing. You may already possess one or more of these three key skills—using ski design to guide the arc of the turn; a bomb-proof parallel start through early weight shift; and finally, dynamic anticipation—but I would still recommend that you read these three chapters in order. Chapter four, on dynamic anticipation, is the most important chapter of the whole book; just as dynamic anticipation itself is the watershed skill that divides fine skiers from mediocre ones. I strongly urge reading this chapter twice. The skill is a subtle one. But, of course, mastering it also depends on your feeling comfortable with the other skills we'll talk about in chapters two and three.

It's no accident that my companion video-tape, *Breakthrough on Skis: The Video,* focuses exclusively on these three key chapters. This is the crux of the matter, the heart of expert skiing—three steps that will give your skiing a new foundation, a new technical basis, a new ease and efficiency. I should tell you that the order of these chapters is no accident either. They build on one another in a way that's both logical and physio*logical.* Don't put the cart before the horse, and risk frustration, by practicing the skills and patterns of chapter four before those of chapter three or two.

Armed with these basic secrets of expert skiing, you should find that your own skiing takes a quantum leap forward. And you'll be ready, at your leisure, to browse through *Part II: The Multiple Worlds of Expert Skiing.* This section is a kind of kaleidoscopic tour of many specialized skiing domains. Don't try to read it, much less absorb it all, straight through. Dip into these chapters as your skiing interests lead you toward one or another of these exciting subworlds of our white universe. . . . Turn to these chapters for hot tips, for an insider's perspective on adapting your advanced technique to special circumstances, for new strategies and relatively painless practice patterns.

It's no accident, however, that the first chapter in Part II is devoted to bumps. Mogul skiing is definitely not everybody's favorite. But it is still the single biggest challenge facing modern skiers, every day, at every ski resort. No matter how polished your technique, you'll never quite believe in yourself as an expert skier until you feel comfortable in the bumps. So although you may be far more tempted, say, by powder, don't neglect chapter five and the opportunity to use your new skills to master the meanest bumps.

In general, Part II is meant to serve as your reference library of technical tricks for the separate, specialized worlds of advanced skiing. There's even a chapter (nine) on the ins and outs, rights and lefts, of what's often called recreational or fun racing (NASTAR style). But I should explain why I haven't delved any deeper into ski racing. First, all the best books on skiing to appear in the last ten years have been written by coaches, and are either exclusively or predominantly devoted to racing. In ski writing the all-around recreational skier has always been neglected, the racer well served. Second, and just as important, I'm a ski teacher—not a coach. My life's work has been to produce expert skiers, not racing champions. One should do what one does best. Even so, racing is an integral and thrilling part of our sport, something that has always enriched my skiing experience, and will yours too.

But I figure that many first-time skiers will also get their hands on this book. Not just average beginners but enthusiastic, gung-ho, ambitious beginners who can barely wait to get through the preliminaries and into the wilder realms of expert skiing—the very best kind of beginners! If you're one of these not-yet-skiers, or perhaps a very inexperienced novice, you haven't been neglected. Chapter one, "Basics," is for you. I've followed the same general principles in describing beginning skiing as expert skiing—not telling you everything, but focusing instead on the few key skills and movement patterns that should take you rapidly on to advanced skiing. Chapter one offers a quick path to the intermediate level of skiing by showing you how to avoid the usual bad habits and hangups that keep people intermediates forever. In this chapter I've tried to steer you around the intermediate doldrums altogether. It's not all that hard to pick up advanced skills from the very beginning.

If you're neither a beginner nor a novice but perhaps have friends who are, Chapter one may help you to help them. It's also an effective but not essential introduction to the three all-important chapters that follow. Even experienced skiers will want to read it sooner or later, if only out of simple curiosity. But remember, chapters two, three and four contain the very essence of this book. They fulfill the promise of Part I: *breaking out of the intermediate rut!* You know as well as I do that this rut is a real one. Most skiers on the slopes today are caught in it. That's why I wrote this book and that's probably why you're reading it. And, by the way, breaking the mold should be, can be, and is, more fun than hard work. But in the case of expert skiing, getting there is *not* half the fun; it's only the bare beginning. So let's begin.

BREAKING OUT OF THE INTERMEDIATE RUT

PART ONE

1

BASICS

Getting into Intermediate Skiing with No Bad Habits

Even on your first day on skis, even on your first run down the hill you feel it. Not exactly the thrill of speed, though the wind in your face may have something to do with it. It is more a strange new kind of freedom. Freedom from what? For one thing, freedom from weight, from effort, or the need to make an effort in order to move swiftly. Freedom from the universal speed limits imposed on everyday life by the laws of gravity and inertia, by our earthbound evolution. For a brief moment or two, you're flying. Then the exhilaration wanes, because, like all of us, you want more. All around you other skiers, better skiers, are also flying—but faster and more gracefully. Why not you?

The notion of intermediate skiing is the starting point for this whole book. Everyone seems to know what I mean when I say "intermediate skiing." I mean ho-hum, so-so skiing, skiing the way most skiers do: not too good, not too bad, a kind of functional but sloppy and relatively graceless way of moving on skis.

This level of skiing can be pure frustration if you've been skiing that way for years and years. But it's also something to be proud of if you were a rank beginner only a week ago. To tell the truth, nobody stays a beginner for long nowadays. One week on skis, or a few weekends in a row, give most folks the confidence and technique to get down the majority of slopes in one piece, more or less under control, and usually smiling. Ours is an age of almost instant intermediate skiing.

But most skiers remain intermediates forever. One reason, of course, is that they often don't know where to go or what to do next—and that's what we'll tackle together in chapters two, three and four. But an equally important reason for this stagnation is that many skiers reach the intermediate plateau by a series of shortcuts. These do indeed produce a rough-and-ready, skidded or "christy" style of skiing, and they do it fast. But they totally neglect the development of a number of key skills that would have allowed such skiers to keep on progressing.

It doesn't have to be this way. Without spending—or wasting—any more time, new skiers can follow a slightly different learning path as they develop the habits of christy-style skiing. An equally simple but more promising route to the intermediate level that will facilitate further progress instead of blocking it is what this chapter is all about. It is a rapid mini-course in the basics of modern skiing for inexperienced skiers—beginners or novices—that

I promise will keep you from falling into all the classical traps. For the majority of my readers —already strong intermediate skiers, I'm sure —this chapter can still be useful, and will offer insights into why the rest of the book works so well. But if you're in a hurry and already a fairly good skier, simply skip these pages and start with chapter two.

Trust Your Skis, Feel Your Feet
Everyone starts skiing in a wedge. Even non-skiers know what a wedge is—that funny V-shaped position with ski tips pointing in and ski tails pushed out. The wedge is both an aid —the skier's equivalent of training wheels, since it offers an easy way to brake, stop and turn—and a hangup. But it's also something more, a sort of stable triangular test platform where beginners (and occasionally experts too) can try out and experiment with key movements and sensations at slow speeds. And it's in a wedge that I want to introduce you to the two most important concepts in modern skiing.

First, *modern skis are designed and built to turn for you.* They need only be guided, not forced, into and through each turn. That's why modern skis cost so much, and also why they're worth every penny. The whole point of ski design today (which will be discussed in more detail later) is to create skis that tend to turn on their own. Ultimately, all the skier has to do is stand on them correctly, precisely and comfortably to let them "do their own thing"

—that is, let them turn for you. At most, the skier needs to make only small guiding adjustments and offer helpful hints to modify or amplify the ski's own built-in tendency to turn. Skiers no longer have to wrestle their skis around corners with brute strength. And this built-in turn is perhaps more obvious and easiest to feel in a wedge.

The second concept, equally important, is equally simple. Today *we ski with our feet.* Not with our shoulders, torsos, hips, arms or knees, but with our feet! It's logical. The foot is the only part of the skier's body in contact with the ski. If you want to guide, edge, twist, weight or unweight your ski, then clearly you must guide, edge, twist, weight or unweight the foot that's attached to it. Certainly in some situations skiers will use the leverage of a bent knee to amplify the movements of their feet. But don't put the cart before the horse; the foot comes first.

Not only do we act on the ski with our feet, but skilled skiers also feel the ski's response through their soles. It's a two-way street. Does this sound strange? Perhaps; but it's important. So right from the very start I want you to pay special attention to your feet, to become aware of them and of what they're doing, of how they feel, of the movement, force and pressure down there. That's where all the real action in skiing takes place. Start making friends with your feet, tuning in to pressure changes across your soles from your very first day on skis. You'll be way ahead of the game if you do.

How do these ideas relate to the wedge? Like this. The real action of wedging involves turning your feet (toes in, heels out) while pressing down and out (pushing the heels of your feet out to the side). Foot action, not your leg or body, creates the wedge. It is the same with turning. If we turn one foot just slightly more than the other and press down on it slightly harder, that ski seems to come alive, to dominate the wedge, and to lead us around in a turn. Think of turning as sending a signal to your ski through your foot.

Of course beginners manage to discover dozens of ways of getting around corners in a wedge, most of which are awkward: too much body English, too much oomph, too much force. It's astonishing how little it takes to make the skis respond and turn for you. A bit more twisting or steering of one foot, a bit more pressure on it, and the turn will simply happen.

I've just mentioned two aspects of turning. There are many ways of describing or of thinking about these two complementary ways of guiding a ski. You can think of *steering* your foot, or simply of *wedging* it a bit more. Likewise, you can think of *shifting weight* from one foot to the other, or of *pushing down* harder on one foot. In a wedge, either of these two actions—pivoting one foot more, or pressing on it more—is sufficient to create some sort of gentle turn. At first you will naturally have a better feeling for one move or the other, but try as soon as possible to feel and apply both together. The combination of pressure and a gentle twist makes the ski want to turn for you much more effectively than either one alone.

Let me clarify one point. When turning, one foot (and one ski) will always be more important than the other. This is more obvious in a wedge than in any other position, for each of the two skis points in a different direction. The right ski aims left, while the left ski aims right. If you want to head left, you must press and twist the ski that is already aimed that way. Then it will dominate and lead you where you want to go. Skiers have a particular way of talking about this dominant ski in a turn, referring to it as the *outside ski*. Why? Because if you think of the turn as a circle or arc on the snow, then the dominant foot and ski are always on the *outside* of the circle. It's confusing at first, but this way of talking about turns is so widespread that you can't escape it. Better go with the flow. Now you'll know what I mean when I say the *the outside foot steers or guides the turn.*

What, exactly, should a novice skier concentrate on while skiing around in a wedge? Not much. Enjoy the newness of it all, savor the fact that wedge turns work so easily, and from time to time try to get right into your feet. Are you standing more on your heels than on your toes? More flat-footed? Are you standing and pressing equally on the soles of both feet? Most of the time, or only between turns? Remember that there are no right answers at this point, only new sensations to explore, identify and refine. Every time you steer a turn, you'll probably do it a bit differently. It's an on-going experiment; you can only find out through experience how much or how little you need to guide that outside foot of the wedge, and how much or how little you need to press down on that turning ski for a certain result at a certain speed.

At this point the only other advice I have for brand-new skiers consists of a few tips for better balance: Stand tall rather than hunched over or crouched down. Spread your arms a little to the side and somewhat in front of you, compensating with them as your balance changes, much like a tightrope walker, or as a kid balancing on a fence would use his arms for balance. And make sure that the newness of your ski boots doesn't cause you to stiffen your ankles. Flexed ankles are a must for good balance at every level of skiing. To avoid stiff ankles, don't buckle the tops of your boots tightly; you might even try putting a bit of foam-rubber padding behind the boot tongue during your first few days of skiing. (If your shins get sore, you'll tend to stiffen your ankles, backing away from the tongue of the boot.)

That's all there is to it—for now, anyway. Your balance will get better and better as you challenge yourself with progressively harder moves on skis.

Spontaneous Christies
So how long are you going to spend skiing around in a wedge, before starting to skid

gracefully around corners with your skis together—or at least parallel—the way most other skiers on the hill do? It all depends. Some skiers start making these *christies,* as such parallel skids are called, after only a couple of hours on skis; others may take a day or two. It all depends on how fast you become truly comfortable in your wedge.

Comfort is the keynote, and here's why. As a beginner you tend to steer your skis rather hard—to oversteer them, really—when you turn. This is quite normal; who knows what these slippery characters might do? This is what I mean by overcontrolling or oversteering the ski—directing every moment, every inch of the ski's circular path in the snow with a tight, active foot. The essence of christy-style skiing, however, which opens the door to both intermediate and advanced technique, is exactly the opposite; it's *letting go!* Letting go of your skis in the sense of directing them less forcefully, allowing them to brush or slip across the snow; and discovering as you do so that the skis keep on turning virtually by themselves. I sometimes refer to the whole process of developing a christy as "making friends with your skis." It sounds corny, but fundamentally it's accurate. Keep in mind that this next phase won't really work unless you feel comfortable on your skis.

There's a kind of backdoor to christy turns that we'll try first. It's cheating really, doing them without properly learning how, which is often the best way to get started with anything

FIG. 1.1 A SPONTANEOUS CHRISTY. *Greater speed and a narrower wedge often result in a natural or spontaneous skid. The inside ski drifts off its edge and parallel to the outside ski, so that the turn ends as a christy without the skier having consciously "closed" that inside ski. A nice introduction to christy-style skiing.*

new. To make it happen you have to be on the right terrain—a wide open, gentle, friendly hill, a place you've skied before, where you feel totally at home in your wedge. Maybe even a slope that feels a bit *too* flat for you. Since it's so easy, I want you to ski a little faster. To do this, simply keep the shape of your wedge very small, barely opening the tails of your skis outward. At the same time, don't rush around those corners as you zigzag your way down the slope. Stretch each turn out into a long round arc, savor it and let it go on and on as you pick up a little more speed than normal in your mini-wedge.

What happens? As a result of skiing faster in a narrower wedge and with a longer turn, your skis will tend to break loose from their normal track, and you'll feel yourself drifting sideways across the snow as you finish the turn. A new sensation—and a delicious one—that is, providing you're already feeling secure, comfortable and well-balanced on your skis. Which is exactly why I asked you to try this experiment on an easy slope.

This drifting, brushing or skidding across the slope is the basis of all the turns we call christies. After you've experienced it once or twice, you'll notice that this gentle skid doesn't stop or interfere with your turn; in fact, the skis seem to turn easier once they've broken free of their edges and started to drift on the snow. There's a simple explanation for this, and it will help you to understand and pursue the christy style of skiing.

The more you wedge, the more you edge, and vice versa. What I mean is that as you widen your wedge, bracing against both skis, the skis tilt up on their edges more and more. This isn't necessarily bad, at least for stopping, since it was the scraping of the edges against the snow that provided your first means of braking on skis. But at the same time, the more your edges bite into the snow, the harder it is for you to steer your skis into a new direction. This is why I've encouraged you to *narrow* your wedge when turning: the two skis will lie much flatter on the snow. Flat enough so that eventually the force of the turn will overpower them and they'll break away to slide sideways, laterally, as you finish the arc. During this sliding or skidding, your skis remain flat on the snow, so the steering action that made the turn happen in the first place seems to be even more effective than normal. Again, *the flatter the ski, the less it resists turning!*

This gives a further clue about facilitating and developing the spontaneous christy I've just described. Keep your feet and ankles as loose and relaxed inside your boots as possible. There are a lot of different ways to make the skis' edges bite into the snow, but the most universal and fundamental way is to stiffen the foot and ankle. So by relaxing feet and ankles, you make your skis lie as flat as possible, even in a gentle, narrow wedge. As a result, they will tend to break into a skid earlier in the turn, or perhaps with even less speed.

A bit more speed was an important part of my recipe for your first spontaneous christies. More speed means more force, force that actually pushes you to the outside of a turn. It is called centrifugal force, and is experienced by anyone moving quickly around a turn: car drivers, motorcyclists, bicyclists—and, of course, skiers. This force due to speed is what actually makes the skis break away sideways into their christy skid. Naturally, the flatter and "looser" your skis are upon the snow, the less you will need to rely on extra speed and force to create the christy.

Now the christy, or skidded turn, is with you to stay! Henceforth, virtually every turn on skis will involve some degree of slipping or skidding sideways—sometimes very slight, but almost always there. So the skier's real task at this point is to get used to this new sensation and develop it to the point where it becomes second nature. Like everything I'm going to talk about in this book, this can only happen through repetition—lots and lots of it. To me, repetition sounds more attractive than the idea of practice, though they're almost the same thing. If something feels good, it's probably fun to repeat it; while practice usually suggests an onerous task. Be that as it may, one or two christies won't do much for your skiing, but hundreds of them will.

One-Legged Skiing

But just as you suspected, there's more to the christy style of skiing than I've let on. Sneaking yourself into spontaneous christies will not in itself make you or anyone into a strong intermediate skier. There is something more subtle and more fundamental about a good christy than just feeling your skis break away in a sideways skid. A christy is the beginning of one-legged skiing. The idea of turning on one foot rather than two is so important that I'm going to take a minute to explain it in detail.

Consider our old friend, the wedge turn, where the outside ski seems to be doing most of the work. The inside ski, on the other hand, appears to *oppose* the progress of the turn. If anything hangs up, catches or blocks the turn it will always be the inside ski; it is, after all, pointed in the opposite direction. If it turns at all, it's only because the inside foot and leg steer it actively into the turn—overcoming its ornery tendency to block a change of direction—or, more likely, because it's flat enough on the snow that it doesn't dig in and get in the way.

With this in mind, you can see more clearly what happens in a spontaneous christy. As the skier steers a relaxed baby wedge into a turn, say to the left, the speed and outward pressure build up until actually only *one* ski, the inside or left ski, breaks loose and skids, sliding out of its wedge to become more or less parallel to the outer ski which, we are surprised to discover, has been skidding around the corner all along. This gives us a new insight into christies in general, and lets us go

FIG. 1.2 TRAVERSING ON ONE SKI. Probably the best way to develop that special sense of one-legged balance so essential to advanced skiing. Play with one ski in the air, moving it up and down, in and out, as you ride the other ski across the hill.

beyond spontaneous christies—the christy as an unplanned "happening"—so that we can start a christy whenever, wherever and at whatever speed we like. The idea is simple. Stand solidly on one foot (the outside foot of the turn) and with the other foot, now freed of your weight, move the inside ski parallel with its mate so that it too can skid.

Surprisingly, a great number of skiers never make this connection. They never make the transition from standing solidly on both feet, as beginners do, to an essentially one-footed, one-legged stance—and their skiing suffers from it. In fact, real progress is as good as over for such skiers. They can and do continue to improve, making faster and better christies, and eventually real parallel turns. But their two-footed, even-weighted stance is a kind of hidden flaw, an anchor holding them back. Such skiers never realize the maximum performance from their skis, nor real ease and freedom. Let's make sure this doesn't happen to you.

What I'm suggesting is that to really pass from the beginning stages of skiing to its upper levels, you must develop a new style of balance: a comfortable stance over one leg, one foot, one ski. Fortunately, we're not planning to ski down a whole mountain, much less one of those steep blue or black runs you've been eyeing, all on one leg. The style of skiing we're about to develop, like the walking, running and skipping we've done all our lives, involves an alternation of support from one leg to the other. But it's not 100 percent natural, because the skier gets on one foot and stays on it for a while—through the whole turn—before shifting weight back to the other foot. In effect, it is a kind of extremely slow-motion walking.

Still, while you're balanced on one foot, a lot can happen that might threaten your stability, so before going on to see what you can do on only one foot, and why your turns will be so much better for it, let me explain how you can get comfortable in this new stance.

In addition to going straight down the slope and turning from side to side, you've also figured out by watching other skiers that it's possible to cross a slope diagonally in long zigzags (called traverses). Choosing the angle of your traverse—either more down the hill, or more across it—controls the speed of your descent. In the old days instructors and students alike would work for hours or even weeks to master a formal and rather pointless traverse position. But all you need to remember, during these zigs and zags down the slope, is to keep your uphill ski tip slightly ahead of the other one. That way they can't cross!

But now I'm going to ask you to traverse on one ski. More specifically, I'd like you to zig and zag back and forth across a comfortable slope standing only on your downhill ski (that means a different foot in each direction) while lifting your uphill ski slightly off the snow. Raise it just enough so that you know you're not using it for support. You'll feel awkward the first time you try this, but it won't last. In a

FIG. 1.3 SKIING WITH WEIGHT SHIFT VS. SKIING ON BOTH SKIS. *The more you weight the outside ski, the more positive an arc it will make. Typically, turns made on two equally weighted skis tend to become sideways, drifting skids.*

few minutes your body will adjust itself, shifting imperceptibly and unconsciously over the downhill ski, and the wobbliness will disappear.

Play with this one-footed traversing. Make a real game out of it. Lift that uphill ski higher, then lower it, twist it from side to side as you cross the slope, lift the tail of the ski more than the tip and vice versa. If you distract yourself from the problem of balancing, paradoxically your balance will improve that much faster. My only two specific balancing suggestions are repeats of my advice a few pages ago: use your arms, spread and advanced, as balancing outriggers and stand with relaxed, *flexed* ankles. This is advice worth repeating because stiff ankles are the number one cause of bad balance among skiers at all levels.

I've asked you to traverse exclusively on your downhill ski. Actually, you can balance across the slope on your uphill ski as well. And for variety, why not? But you'll find that traversing on the downhill ski comes closest to the type of one-legged balance you'll need and use in harder skiing. And as soon as you begin to feel fairly stable on one ski, you can put this new skill, this new form of balance, right to use to improve your christies. Using that mini-wedge, start into a complete turn: down the hill, then back across. But now, as you pass the halfway point of your turn, shift solidly onto the outside ski and balance on it exclusively as you complete the turn. What happens? The other ski, lighter now, breaks into its parallel skidding action much more easily and sooner than before. Or at least it should.

Most people execute a better christy when they add *weight shift*. However, it may not help everyone, because the turn I've just suggested is only an improved version of the spontaneous christy—improved by weight shift so that the lightened inside ski can drift off its edge into a skid more easily. There are some skiers for whom the spontaneous christy doesn't seem to work well—primarily skiers with stiff, tight legs, or those with knock-knees. If you fit this description, you'll have to add one last element to your turns to achieve a really satisfying, smooth and graceful christy. Even so, weight shift—that is, placing yourself solidly on the outside ski of the turn —is still essential, so we're on the right track.

For all of you who can feel a real difference as you balance more and more completely on the outside ski of the turn, great! Keep it up. See if you can't shift onto that outside ski even earlier in the turn, virtually as soon as you open your skis into that mini-wedge. The sooner the better, for the earlier your weight shift, the earlier the christy phase will start, and the more time you spend in that delicious (and ultimately more efficient) parallel skid, the less time you'll be in a wedge.

Inside Leg Action
Even hot shots and naturals, as well as those who don't take so readily to spontaneous

christies, have one last key movement pattern to learn at this stage of their skiing careers. I call it *inside leg action.*

Making the turn happen is basically the job of the outside leg, foot and ski. The role of the inside leg is to smooth the turn out and make it flow. Suppose only one leg is active; a wedge results. If you want your turn to continue as a christy, it's up to the other foot and leg to take that ski which isn't helping, make it light and gently shift or steer it parallel to the active ski. This is inside leg action.

It's a whole lot more than just jerking that inside ski off the snow and slamming it in parallel to the other ski. This is a popular misconception and a terrible hangup to get rid of later on. The real motion is smooth and subtle, and does several things at once. The inside ski is lightened, rolled off any edge it may have, and gently eased in parallel to—but not really touching—the other ski. Since only the tails of the skis are spread in a wedge, the skier has the feeling of actively moving *only the heel of his inside foot* in order to roll the ski in parallel. In reality, the entire leg helps, but it's always a good idea to focus one's attention on what the foot is doing.

Here, for the first time, I've started to explain something that sounds complicated. It isn't really. But to keep things simple, let's get away from theory and description and look at a couple of simple skiing games with which you can get a feeling for inside leg action. First, just wedge straight down a gentle slope,

not even turning. Then try to pull your weight off one ski, lightening it as much as possible. Surprise! Your wedge will turn. Also, you will have felt how lightening one ski is the exact equivalent of pressing down on the other—opposite sides of the same coin, so intimately related that it doesn't really matter whether you think of getting *onto* the outside ski, or of getting *off* the inside one. It's all the same.

Next, repeat the experiment, wedging straight down the hill (this straight-down direction is known as the fall line). But this time flatten one ski out on the snow as much as you can (primarily by relaxing your ankle, but if necessary by rolling your knee out a little). Once again your wedge will begin to turn toward the flat ski, only this time you probably won't be so surprised. What have you learned? That reducing resistance (edging) on the inside of an intended turn allows the outside ski to do its thing. What else? Usually when I ask skiers to try these experiments, not only a turn, but a spontaneous christy results. In other words, by reducing the weight and grip of the inside ski, it's much more likely to drift in parallel for a christy skid.

Now we'll guarantee the christy effect by not only flattening and lightening the inside ski—relaxing and flexing the whole inside leg is a good way of doing this—but at the same time gently pivoting that heel in so that it is parallel to the other foot. This is the whole package of movement that I've labeled inside leg action. It should rapidly become second nature—the sooner the better—and is actually part of the basic technique of all advanced skiers, whether instructors or Olympic competitors.

Like many critical elements of modern ski technique, inside leg action is not just one move but an integrated pattern in which the body, or part of the body, does several things at once. In this case, the inside leg lightens and flattens the inside ski of the turn while pivoting it. Contrast this with the role of the outside leg. As you learned earlier in this chapter (see "Trust Your Skis, Feel Your Feet"), the outside leg pivots or steers its ski while pressing down on it. There's a cooperative effort in the ideal ski turn in which each leg (or foot) has a different role and responsibility. Fortunately you can master these integrated leg actions separately, slowly, patiently, and then combine them to achieve the complementary leg action of modern skiing. Fortunately too, the physical experience is always simpler and easier than any written description can suggest.

So far I've been talking almost interchangeably about your foot and leg. Technically, the leg is involved in every movement pattern I've described, but first and foremost you should be aware of what your foot is doing and what it feels like. With enough mileage, patience and concentration you will actually be able to feel what your skis are doing by the way your feet feel. More than any other part of the body, *your feet are where the action is in skiing.* This is true even though your leg often must move too in order to help the foot do its job.

This is nowhere more evident than with knock-kneed skiers—and many skiers, especially women (with their different pelvic structure and looser joints), are quite knock-kneed. Such skiers find that in a wedge their skis are more on edge than they would like, and consequently that it's difficult to pivot the inside ski parallel in order to trigger the christy phase of a turn. What to do? Simply concentrate on rolling your knee *out* as you pivot your heel *in* toward the other foot. This outward flexing of the knee and bent leg (as though, for a second, you were trying to make yourself bowlegged instead of knock-kneed) will flatten the ski so that it will slide in parallel to the other one quite easily. Yet another way to visualize this action is to think of rolling the inside knee in the direction of the turn.

Perhaps before we leave this subject to hit the slopes, it might be helpful to practice this inside leg action at home. Sitting in a chair with your feet on the floor in a slight wedge position, imagine that you're making a turn to the left. Your left foot would be the inside foot, so simply lighten it on the floor and pivot the heel in parallel to the right foot. This is the inside leg action that triggers a christy to the left. (Of course, on skis you would be standing up, relaxed and tall.) Try this movement a few more times, and as your foot pivots, note how easy it is to help it by rolling your knee out as well. This accompanying knee action is probably always a part of effective inside leg action, but only knock-kneed skiers really need to become aware of it.

Enough for now. We eased our way into christy skiing by simply skiing faster in a smaller wedge, letting the extra force push us into a parallel skid. Next we learned to balance on the outside ski, taking pressure off the inside one to facilitate its moving parallel (i.e., matching or closing). Finally, to trigger the christy phase at will, we learned to gently steer that inside ski in parallel, once the weight was off it. Altogether we've accomplished a great deal, and the result of all this is a solid smooth christy that is not far from an advanced parallel turn.

Of course, if a christy were just a turn that ends with both skis skidding parallel, it wouldn't be necessary to deal with all these extra skills: weight shift, one-legged balance, inside leg action. The christy we care about is less the typical intermediate's turn than a package of skills that can take us much further —clear into expert skiing. All too many skiers tend to stop once they've achieved some sort of basic approximation of a skidded turn (what we've called a spontaneous christy). They rest on their laurels or, more accurately, go off and boogy until their rough-and-ready, jerky version of a christy becomes a deeply ingrained habit. That's too bad, for changing habits is a lot harder than forming good ones in the first place.

If you are a wedge-turning beginner just getting into christies, you should do a lot of skiing. If you use this chapter for guidance, you'll be building up classical skiing patterns that will take you a long way. The progress and the skills I've described represent several days on the slopes. A functional christy of any sort will get you off beginners' green runs and onto many intermediate blues. Not too steep at first, please, and not bumpy. Immediately and intuitively you will experience a greater sense of security and more control with a christy than with a wedge. But what next?

You have now entered the vast and nebulous world of intermediate skiing. It's an exciting world indeed, if you're just getting there: new slopes, new shapes, new dimensions to explore. Mileage will do wonders for your technique. Almost at once you'll begin to adapt your new christy to different slopes: steering harder, skidding around faster when the slope seems steep and narrow, relaxing and drifting in bigger arcs when the pressure's off. No two christies will be exactly the same —nor should they be. You'll soon find that the wedgelike start of your christy becomes less and less important; the graceful skidded arc will take up more and more of the turn. Each day on the slopes will add to your confidence, and skiing will become easier—and more fun —than you ever imagined.

All the same, intermediate skiing can turn into a trap, a world of frustration if you remain there too long. The next three chapters are devoted to helping you out of the intermediate plateau. Still, if you get a handle on one-legged balance and inside leg action in the beginning, you'll probably never get stuck in this rut at all. For now, congratulations! Enjoy your handsome new skidded christies to the full . . . And make a few good ones for me.

- *Modern skis are designed and built to turn on their own, with minimal force and effort on the part of the skier.*

- *The feet are the most important part of the skier's body: all input to the skis must pass through them, and much feedback also reaches you through the soles of your feet. Tune in to your feet!*

- *In wedge turns, combine increased pressure on one leg with a gentle steering motion of the same foot; that ski dominates and steers the wedge in a turn.*

- *To achieve a spontaneous christy, ski faster, use a narrower wedge and steer it in a longer turn.*

- *For a more sophisticated, efficient christy, learn to stand completely on the outside ski. Develop this one-footed stance and one-legged balance by practicing traverses on one ski.*

- *Smooth out your christies with inside leg action, flexing the inside leg to lighten the inside ski and bringing it parallel with the active, weighted outside ski.*

2

THE ARC OF THE TURN

Using Ski Design Rather Than Brute Force to Complete Turns

Something there is about turns . . . the sweep and dash, the grace and rhythm, the endless speeding up and slowing down. The narrow saves where you barely turn out of a disaster. Those special turns that seem to happen by themselves. The hundreds and hundreds of turns you make each day you ski, the millions you perform in a skiing lifetime. Then one day it clicks: skiing *is* turning. Without turns this sport of ours wouldn't exist. And almost as an afterthought, comes the big picture. On skis, turns are more, much more, than changes of direction. They express *you* as a skier. They express your moods, your instincts, your personality—lazy and relaxed, or dynamic and aggressive. They express your level of confidence or anxiety. The speed, the precision, the spontaneity, the flow, the very shape of turns, all these tell us something about the skier. Particularly their shape. Round graceful arcs are the characteristic signature that expert skiers inscribe on their white canvas. Jerky, sharp corners are a dead giveaway of those who haven't yet made peace with their skis. Great turns, great arcs on the snow require a real collaboration between skis and skier, man and material. They are also, for many skiers, a mystery.

You probably consider yourself an intermediate skier—perhaps even the quintessential intermediate—or you wouldn't be reading this chapter. But just what does such a label mean? Well, for one thing, it means you're a pretty fair skier: comfortable and relaxed on easy slopes, confident of your ability to get down most moderate slopes, but still with large gaps in your skiing repertoire, many areas of frustration. On a sunny day, skiing groomed runs that aren't too steep, you experience sublime moments when it seems the whole mountain belongs to you. All the money you've spent on equipment, lift tickets, condominium lodging, the "whole catastrophe" as Zorba put it, seems worthwhile, even cheap. But there are other nagging times when you find yourself on a slope where you feel you don't belong, say in the middle of a field of icy moguls, when you curse under your breath and wonder why you ever took up this silly sport in the first place.

Worse yet, if you're a dyed-in-the-wool intermediate, you've probably been skiing like this for quite a while. Set in your ways. The days of heady progress are long since past and don't look like they'll ever come again. Technically, you probably make a sort of inconsistent and sloppy parallel turn (maybe "parallelish" describes it better). When the slope is easy, you turn both skis and skid easily around the corner. But you're conscious of lacking some indefinable grace—something you'd probably call good form without being 100 percent sure what good form really is. When the slopes get steeper, tougher, narrower or bumpier, the parallel quality of your turn tends to disappear. You spread or stem your uphill ski out into the turn (maybe just a wee bit), pulling the other one after it at the last minute, and generally horsing your skis around the corner. On really tough slopes each turn is a crisis, never a pleasure, and you wind up wrestling with your skis instead of riding them. And you don't like it one bit. You've got the intermediate blues.

What's wrong? Well, the vast majority of skiers in this situation are turning too hard—using too much muscular force to twist their skis—and getting very little benefit from the ski design itself in each turn. I propose that in this chapter we're going to make friends with our skis. We're going to learn to let the ski do most of the work for us. And we're going to learn to trust our skis to complete each turn on their own. *Completing each turn* is the important idea here. It's not so important at first to improve the parallel start of our turns—that can come later. Rather, we'll concentrate on the round arc of each turn, especially the tail end; and make sure that these arcs (ninety percent of each turn really) are the result of ski design interacting with snow, and not of brute force. It's partly a case of getting all you paid for out of your skis. The hypothetical intermediate I described above—and that means the great majority of skiers—might just as well be skiing on old wooden boards (two-by-fours, if you like) for all the good he's getting out of his sleek modern skis.

Getting the Ski to Do the Job

So let's begin. Like most skiers, you probably shift your weight to the outside ski at the start of each turn. And like most skiers—either through laziness, imperfect balance, or simply because no one ever showed you otherwise— you then let a lot of your body weight fall back onto the inside ski. So you actually make most of the turn on both feet. No more! I want you to get *completely* onto that *outside* ski and stay there, balanced on it for the entire turn. No kidding. I'm talking about developing a style of one-footed skiing. A surprising suggestion to many, I realize, since the fact that experts make every turn virtually on one foot must surely be one of the best-kept secrets of modern skiing.

Admittedly, it doesn't look as though we are skiing on one foot. When you watch a hot skier—instructor, coach, racer, whatever—you see two parallel skis carving the arc of each turn. What you don't see is that the inside ski of the turn is completely weightless, floating along on the snow next to the outside ski, which is really carrying the skier. Often the

FIG. 2.1 SKI DESIGN, HOW IT WORKS. *Two separate effects due to ski design tend to make the ski turn. The carving effect, illustrated at the top, relies on the curved waist of the ski—and on the ski being weighted and bent to accentuate this curve. The skidding effect, shown at the bottom, is due to greater friction or gripping at the wide tip of the ski. In practice, the two effects always work together but generally one or the other predominates, leading to a more or less carved, or more or less skidded, turn. Note that carving is a function of edge angle—the greater the ski's angle, the shorter a turn it will carve—but skidding does not depend on the angle of the edge.*

light inside ski *is* lifted a tad, a smidgen, a centimeter or so off the snow. But generally no higher since that ski won't get any lighter even if it's hoisted a visible foot or so off the snow. Lifting the inside ski visibly off the snow takes extra effort and can only compromise your balance. And so this critical aspect of modern skiing remains more or less hidden, almost invisible. The best skiers are skiing exclusively on one foot. Period. And you should too.

I said this was one of the best-kept secrets of modern skiing. Is it then an especially modern phenomenon? Haven't the best skiers always skied on their outside ski? The truth is: not as much as we do today. This aspect of expert technique has only become so important in recent years because of changes in ski design and construction. All modern skis are softer flexing than they were ten or even five years ago. Time was when, in order to build a ski that would hold well on hard or icy snow, manufacturers had to stiffen the entire ski. Torsional stiffness (resistance to bending around the long axis of the ski), which makes the ski grip and hold, was almost impossible to separate from stiffness in flex (bending underfoot). Only in recent generations of skis have engineers learned to build a soft-flexing ski that is still torsionally rigid enough for high performance. Net result: Our modern skis really do bend into a curve underfoot when we weight them. This curve is called reverse camber, and it contributes enormously to the modern turn.

FIG. 2.2 RIDING A BENT SKI. *The more a skier is able to ride exclusively on the outside ski, the less need there is for muscular twisting to complete the turn.*

For this reason, I want you to stand with all your weight on the outside ski in each and every turn. If you stand on one foot instead of two, you'll be doubling the weight on that foot. And with twice as much weight available to bend that ski underneath you, you naturally get the maximum reverse camber out of your ski. What happens? In addition to the normal skidding effect in your turns, the bent ski will want to follow its own curve along the snow—introducing more of a carved effect. As your ski follows its own arc around the turn, you will have the impression of doing less work for more turn than ever before.

Hasn't this always been possible? Didn't Jean-Claude Killy carve his turns with reverse-cambered skis to a triple Olympic victory back in '68? Indeed he did. But the average skier of that period couldn't carve. On earlier skis, such reverse-camber bending was possible only at racing speeds (25, 30 mph and up), and even then only when the skier really stomped on his outside ski. Nowadays, with our incredible softer flexing (yet still torsionally stiff) skis, simply standing on the outside ski is sufficient to bend it into reverse camber and, *voilà,* that ski really starts to perform. Conversely, if you let your weight fall back off that outside ski so that, in essence, you're turning on both feet, your ski will lose that all important reverse bend and straighten out. You'll find yourself skidding sideways when you could be carving a beautiful arc in the snow.

Why Round Turns? The Control Factor

Let's talk about arcs for a minute. Really good skiers, experts, don't skid sideways around the corner, but instead carve clean round arcs in the snow with every turn. But let's not go overboard. Every good turn has some skidding and some carving in it; after all, our skis are not razor blades. Yet almost every really advanced turn describes a round arc in the snow, the skis coming cleanly around in a circle. A far cry from the typical twist/skid movement of the intermediate that produces a much sharper, more abrupt form of cornering. S's versus Z's if you will. But why? Why are round arcs in the snow so important to top skiers?

It is not, believe me, because of some obscure geometrical or aesthetic fascination with round shapes. The answer has to do with control and with braking—the easy way. Control in skiing means two things: control of your direction, and control of speed. Obviously, guiding your skis in positive round arcs is one way of controlling your direction—but the real importance of a round turn has to do with speed control. Consider a moment that every time you turn downhill, you speed up. In the first half of every turn, your skis go from a traverse (safe) to the real angle of the slope (steep). Result: acceleration. Everyone feels this, even first-day beginners. And so in the second half of the turn, you've got to slow down. Either that or face the unpleasant prospect of accelerating endlessly from turn to turn.

What are the options? Only two. A crude way of slowing down is to brace your skis across your direction of travel and scrape off some of that speed. Beginners do this in a wedge. Intermediates do the same thing by twisting their skis sideways (overpivoting), then scraping the snow as they skid sideways through the second half of the turn (the deadly twist/skid pattern). And it works, but crudely. Not only is it hard to judge how much skidding you need to slow down, but also in skidding your legs act like shock absorbers, soaking up all that excess energy of movement. And they'll feel mighty tired at the end of the day.

But I mentioned two options. The second, more sophisticated way to slow down is to use the terrain. Imagine skiing into a hollow gully and up the other side. The change of slope, from steep to flat to uphill, would slow you right down—not the force of your own legs. This is exactly what the skier does who guides his skis in round arcs down the mountain. As the ski carves an arc, it will naturally accelerate into the fall line. But then, coming slowly around the arc from the fall line to the horizontal, the angle of the slope under the ski flattens out more and more, and eventually even climbs uphill if the skis keep on arcing around past the horizontal. In other words, by skiing a round arc, you have created the shape of that hollow gully right there on the slope. And how much you slow down depends only on how far around the arc you come—not on how hard, how violently you turn.

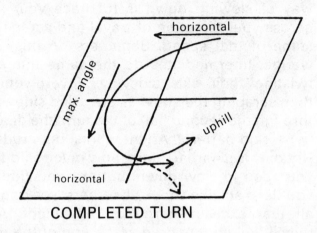

COMPLETED TURN

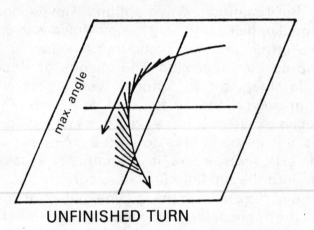

UNFINISHED TURN

FIG. 2.3 ROUND TURNS VS. SKIDDED TURNS FOR BRAKING.
In the upper, round or completed turn, it's the actual shape of the turn—decreasing from steep to horizontal and finally even moving uphill—that slows the skier. In the lower diagram, where the turn is neither rounded nor finished, the skier is obliged to pivot the skis more sideways, and slow down by scraping, using his legs like shock absorbers and paying the price of increased fatigue.

FIG. 2.4: ROUND TURNS VS. SKIDDED TURNS CONTINUED.
The same two approaches to speed control illustrated by the preceding diagram, but shown here with skier's figures. The round turn is a graceful, controlled option. The skidded corner is a violent and fatiguing approach to speed control.

This is what carving—or more precisely, guiding the skis in round arcs—really promises: effective braking without using your leg muscles to resist your speed. The choice is yours. The further around the arc you come, the slower you'll go, because the terrain under your skis will be flattening out. It's easy to maintain a given speed down the hill (whether slow, moderate, or very fast) by patiently remaining in each turn just long enough so that one's exit speed from it is the same as one's entrance speed. Patience—and round turns! And of course, when I talk about remaining in the turn, I mean staying balanced over your *outside* ski. As long as you stay on one foot, the ski keeps turning. The moment your weight falls off onto the inside ski, there goes that reverse-camber bend, and presto, that clean round arc disappears. Now you're starting to see why my idea of skiing on one foot is so important.

The Long and Short of It: Different-Sized Arcs

You're thinking, I know, that it can't be that simple. And you're right. Nothing ever is. But what I've just sketched out is, in general, the way experts get their skis to turn for them (by weighting the outside ski exclusively), and also the way they control their speed (by completing each arc). Now we need to look at subtler factors, some variations on this theme.

So far we've learned that a totally weighted ski bends and follows its own curve in an arc on the snow. But there's one question still crying out to be answered: How can you get the ski to make different-sized arcs in different situations? You've only got so much weight, and putting it all on one ski only gives so much bend, right? And if we were to draw this bend, or reverse camber, out on the snow it would produce only a long, gradual curve. Very nice for cruising on easy slopes, but how about shorter arcs, the ones we need on steeper, tougher slopes?

Not to worry. There are a couple of subtle ways to gain even more control over the arc of the turn, and to shorten it as much as we want. The operative word here is *subtle.* Instinctively, and with no subtlety whatever, average skiers just twist their legs and skis harder when they want to make short turns. Our goal is to get the skis themselves to turn faster—not for the skier to work harder. And all it takes is a little more outside leg action. Like this: While standing on your outside ski, coming around the arc, simply flex that weight-bearing outside leg a bit more, pushing your bent knee forward into the turn. Sure enough, the ski turns faster, the turn shortens.

Why? Well, this outside leg action—flexing the knee forward and in—does two things. It builds up pressure where the wide tip of the ski is gripping the snow. The more the tip grips, the more the tail section slides out sideways; and the ski follows a shorter arc on the snow. But this is only half of the story. For too much of this forward pressing/sinking action can make the tails skid excessively, and then we've lost that wonderful feeling of carving. The other half of the story involves the *inward* movement of leg and knee. What this does is to tilt the ski more on edge. And, luckily, the more the ski is edged, the more reverse camber we can squeeze out of it—which will help us to shorten the turn without excess skidding. The explanation of this little gem of technical insight is not, for once, so simple. Think of your ski tilted up on edge but with no weight on it. Because the center or waist of your ski is narrower than tip and tail, it won't touch the snow. There will be a small gap or hollow spot between the ski's edge (right underfoot) and the snow. When the ski is weighted, the resulting bend brings the edge back in contact with the snow, producing our famous reverse camber. Now the higher the edge angle, the bigger this potential gap and the more room the ski has to bend. In short, the more the ski is edged, the more reverse camber you can squeeze out of it. And the more you can reverse the camber, the shorter a carved turn you can produce.

In practical terms, shortening the natural turning radius of the ski doesn't mean going for all carve or all skid. It's not a matter of merely edging the ski more, or of just flexing that outside leg, or of pushing the bent outside knee into the turn. To make the ski respond faster, you do *all of the above* in a subtle, balanced combination movement: outside leg action. The precision, the feeling, the putting-it-all-togetherness of outside leg action comes from repetition, from experiment, from playing around with it. There are also a few practice tricks that I'll describe in a moment.

The crux of the matter, though, is to flex the outside leg more than normal if you want the ski to react faster than normal. The more you "sink through" the turn on your outside leg, the shorter an arc your ski will make. For you this means freedom. At the very least, freedom from having to overtwist your skis or jerk them around in order to make a short turn. Even very short turns can be started in a relaxed, unhurried, more or less normal way, and then, when you want the ski to come around faster, it's sufficient to flex that outside knee a bit more into the turn and—ah!—the ski obeys and cuts on around twice as fast. You'll notice I've used a lot of different words to describe it: sink, flex, bend the outside leg, press the knee into the turn (forward and in), et cetera. Actually, it's all the same move. But I hope by having used a variety of words that I've conjured up a general, not over-specific image of what the skier must do to make the ski come alive and turn faster.

While I'm at it, let me warn you against a common misinterpretation of this leg action. If you bend nothing but your knee, your hips (your weight) will fall back behind your heels, overloading the tail of the ski—and that beautiful arc will turn into a messy sideways skid. This is why I keep stressing that your knee should flex *forward* in the direction of the turn.

FIG. 2.5: SHORT VS. LONG ARCS. How fast the ski will turn for you depends largely on how much leg action you apply to it. Bending and pressing the outside knee forward and into the turn selectively applies more pressure and more edge to the turning ski—more leg action equals a faster, shorter turn. In the long-radius turn, the skier remains upright and relaxed, a passive passenger on a more slowly turning ski.

That way your ankle will also bend; your weight will remain more centered; and the wide tip of the ski will actually work for you, leading you through the arc. Remember our number one goal: *making the ski do the work, not the skier.*

A final note on the theory, the "why" of controlling the arc of various turns. Don't get hung up worrying about the difference, the dichotomy between skidded and carved turns. Every good turn has some skid and some carve in it. The special quality of modern skis is that today the carved aspect of our turns is greater than ever. Modern ski design puts a bit more carving effect into each turn—that is, as long as you keep standing one hundred percent on that outside ski. Inevitably, as you become a real expert, you will rely more and more on the carved aspect of your turns, and less and less on the skidded aspect. But it's a matter of degree, not an either/or thing.

Making It Happen: Building New Habits

Now you know why the ski turns; how it has been designed to make your life easier; why it's important to *complete* the arc of the turn; and, finally, how you can control what size turn your skis want to make. Great. It's time for some action. Your aim now is to start using ski design instead of your own muscles—and, even more, to make this a habit. A way of skiing that becomes second nature, that you no longer have to think about. Here's the fastest way to do that:

First, divide your skiing time into practice/ learning time and just plain fun-skiing time. No matter how badly you want to become an expert skier, don't make the mistake of trying to practice your new moves all the time. You'll only become bored or frustrated, and it just won't work. But by the same token, unless you put some time aside to concentrate, to ski with focus and attention, to really work on new moves, it won't happen either. Progress in upper-level skiing does not occur by osmosis. An alteration of relaxed with serious skiing—say two runs of concentrated practice, followed by two runs of don't-give-a-damn, let-it-all-out skiing, then a couple more serious practice runs—produces the best results, the fastest progress.

Start practicing on slopes somewhat easier than those you normally ski—wide, easy, open, groomed. The choice of almost trivial terrain frees you to experiment with new movement patterns. And you'll feel no anxiety, conscious or unconscious, about whether those skis are actually going to turn. Remember, your main task is to do far *less* than previously to create and guide a turn. For starters, I want you to spend quite some time skiing big, lazy, round arcs. Don't even think about short turns. You'll learn more and have more time to adjust your new balance on one foot and feel the ski respond in a long-radius turn than in a short one.

So just ski. Smoothly, gently—but above all *on one foot.* Since my suggested practice slopes are easy ones, you won't be tempted to overtwist, or overinitiate your turns. Just shift your weight to the new outside ski and see what happens. . . . You'll experience a slight pause, a delicious instant of hesitation in which you won't really know whether the ski is going to turn. And then, slowly, inevitably, it starts arcing on around. Spend quite a few runs skiing like this, turning *only* through weight shift, to familiarize yourself with the natural-sized turn that the ski seems to make on its own. You'll know you're doing it right if you suddenly have the surprising sensation that you aren't doing anything—that the ski does it all.

Is this difficult to do? Not really. If you've been skiing for years, if you're the plateaued intermediate this book is mainly addressed to, then you certainly have enough balance to ski from foot to foot; it's just that you've never tried it. As I said earlier, the idea of balancing through the whole turn exclusively on the outside foot is one of the best-kept secrets of modern skiing. It's not visually obvious and it's seldom stressed in ski schools.

But suppose you do have a problem. Say, you shift your weight and then, in the middle of a turn, you find yourself suddenly falling back on two skis, skidding sideways instead of arcing cleanly around. Why, then, you'll just have to spend more time developing one-legged balance. No big deal. Use some of the moves I described in chapter one for skiers just starting into christies. Traverse across the slope on one foot, lifting the other foot and ski right off the snow. Play around with them: tip up, tail up, foot out to the side, then back in, all the while in the air. Use the dullest moments of your skiing day to work on one-footed balance: ski across the flats on one foot, down boring catwalks on one foot. You can do it. Remember: unless you can balance comfortably *and exclusively* on one ski in your turns, all your chances of breaking out of the intermediate doldrums go up in smoke. One-footed skiing is not an option, it's a *must*. None of the other elements of advanced technique make sense if you're still skiing packed slopes on two feet.

So let's assume all goes well. You've spent some time on easy slopes, paying your dues, practicing complete weight shift and enjoying the feeling of pure, round, long-radius turns that seem to happen on their own. As soon as all this starts to feel comfortable, natural, then it's time to move on to progressively steeper slopes and to play with shorter turns, smaller arcs. But please, progressively. Don't jump onto steep black slopes and expect to carve clean, round arcs. It won't happen. Your newly formed habit of riding the ski, rather than wrestling it around the corner, will disappear just like that. Ease onto steeper slopes, one notch at a time.

Right away you'll want to guide your skis in smaller turns (to avoid excess speed on these steeper slopes). So you begin to need, and use, some vertical motion over that weighted outside ski. Vertical motion? Just skiers' jargon for that sinking/flexing/forward-knee-pushing action that we now know makes the ski turn faster. But it's not only sinking, for what goes down must come up. First, you stand up on that new ski. Then slowly, smoothly, you sink through the turn on your outside leg—finishing in a lower, more flexed stance than you started with. And then, naturally, you've got to stand *up* once more, in order to get onto the new ski of the next turn. In order to be ready, once more, to flex on down to control the next arc. Hence the idea of vertical motion. You can't keep flexing forever, lower and lower and still lower—but must obviously straighten back up to repeat the process with each new turn.

Now one form of vertical motion or another, these alternating downs and ups, has been part of ski technique for as long as anyone can remember, whether the Latinic *flexion-extension* of the French Alps or the more basic Anglo-Saxon version of *down-hup!-and around.* Only the vertical motion I'm talking about is quite different. For generations, skiers have been rising up in order to facilitate the start of their turns (up-unweighting is the proper term). But we no longer need that strong *up* (at least ninety percent of the time) with our marvelous, soft-flexing modern skis. The active movement for today's skier is the *down*—the flexing/sinking/driving action of the outside knee and leg that controls how fast the ski will turn. The *up* is a simple and relaxed return to a neutral position, nothing more. We've changed the stress in classical vertical motion one-hundred-eighty degrees.

A final tip. In modern ski boots you aren't able to sink very far before your weight starts to fall backward. Maybe only two or three inches of balanced flexing is all you get. Don't use up this limited range of vertical motion too soon in your turn. Time that sinking/flexing/pushing of the outside leg so that you arrive at the bottom of your range of motion just as you get to the end of the turn. A smooth continuous sinking, or "giving" of the leg throughout the arc. Remember, too, the faster you sink, the harder you press your knee forward and in, the faster the ski will respond and turn. So play around with both the timing and the intensity of your outside leg action to get a feeling for how fast your skis will respond. And don't get carried away with this sinking/pressing action. Back off from time to time, especially on gentler slopes and flats, and just shift onto the new ski without any sinking follow-through whatever. The ski, as if on vacation, follows its natural arc in a long-radius turn.

This is the real core, the common thread of everything I've suggested: letting the ski do its thing. More turn for less work. I'm willing to bet that after you've played with this idea for a while, an enormous Cheshire-cat grin will spread over your face. It feels great. It can't really be this easy. It is.

The Inside Leg Revisited:
The Secret of a Narrow Stance

As soon as you start using the natural arc of the ski, riding around each curve balanced exclusively on the outside foot, something interesting happens to your overall stance. Your feet, your skis, start to stay much closer together. The typical wide stance that is one of the hallmarks of the perennially plateaued, two-footed intermediate skier begins to wither away. To be precise, you'll find that the inside ski of each turn, the light one, tends to stay in closer to the active, weighted outside ski. This is a natural, automatic and unconscious happening for at least half the skiers who start to ski more on one foot. And it's all to the good.

You may be wondering why it's so good to ski with your skis closer together, especially since nowadays almost all beginners are taught to ski with their skis apart. Actually, the wide stance for novices is merely a sort of "training wheels" arrangement. It guarantees stability and security, long before the beginner has had time to develop the trickier one-footed balance of advanced skiing. But it more or less condemns one always to bear weight on the inside ski of the turn. And we now know what a disaster, what a can of worms that is.

Granted, expert skiers today make no effort to ski with legs, feet and skis pinched tightly together (a look that typified expert skiers ten to fifteen years ago). To do so would be to lose all independent shock-absorbing potential, all the natural foot-to-foot balance that we've developed throughout our lives. Man is born a biped, not a monoped. But despite that, the best skiers still ski with their skis fairly close together (just how close varies with personal preference and body build). And for good reason. With the skis in a relatively narrow relation, it takes much less effort to shift weight from one foot to the other. And in particularly challenging conditions—such as big bumps and powder—a narrow track is a must. If you ski wide-track in big bumps, for example, you'll find one ski way down in the trough, the other way up on the side of the bump—and you can imagine the resulting struggle. Finally —why not be honest?—not only is it more efficient to ski with your feet more or less close (but remember: not touching!), it also feels and looks more graceful. A narrow stance is part and parcel of the expert's repertoire. It should be part of yours, too.

As I've pointed out, the narrower stance often seems to happen on its own once you begin to ski completely on the outside foot. The light inside ski tends to drift in beside its mate. But not always. If your legs are muscularly tight, or if the habit of making wide-track skidded turns is deeply ingrained, then you'll have to train the inside leg of each turn to behave like the cooperative partner it's supposed to be. (I've already sketched out inside leg action for novices in chapter one; and indeed, many lucky beginners master this movement pattern during their first week on skis. But I want to discuss it here from a more advanced point of view.) Fortunately, what I call inside leg action is anything but difficult.

For starters, simply concentrate on the *heel* of your inside foot and then, as you come smoothly around a long-radius turn on the other, weighted foot, pull that light heel in toward the weighted, outside ski. It's dead easy because your inside foot and ski are bearing no weight. On the other hand, it would be almost impossible to pull or drag the inside ski toward its mate if you were standing squarely on *both* feet (as bad as trying to lift yourself up by your own bootstraps).

Now, this inward pulling of the heel is quite a subtle business. For one thing, the movement is only visible initially, and then only if your skis are spaced rather far apart at the start of the turn. Once you've pulled, or eased, that light ski in next to the turning ski, no inward movement is visible whatsoever. Yet the movement continues. You're still gently controlling the tail of the inside ski with the heel of your foot, through the whole arc of the turn. Think of this action as a kind of isometric exercise: steady, continuous, light muscular effort of that inside heel, yet no visible movement. The ski simply maintains its position next to the turning ski and doesn't drift back apart into a wide stance. Again, you should practice this control of the inside ski on wide gentle slopes in the course of big round turns. It's remarkably easy.

So we've exposed another secret of advanced skiing. An expert's skis don't really just stay there, neatly and closely parallel from turn to turn to turn. Not only do hot skiers shift their weight onto one ski, the outside ski of the turn, but at the same time they pull the light inner ski in close to its fellow, and they *hold it there* through the entire arc. Luckily, this takes hardly any thought. After maybe an hour's practice, it becomes an unconscious habit. Exactly the same way that we constantly wiggle the steering wheel of our car from side to side in order to steer a straight line down the freeway. We aren't conscious of doing it, and are only aware of driving straight. Yet if we stopped this continual adjusting of the wheel, the automobile would quickly leave the road. In a like manner, the accomplished skier is continually (and unconsciously) adjusting the light, inside ski in its position next to the active, turning one. An easy habit to develop, but an all-important one.

Still, this gentle inward pull of the heel is not the whole story of inside leg action. (And please, never attempt to hold your skis close by pinching your knees together or tucking one knee behind the other; this is a disastrous misinterpretation and a terrible, counterproductive legacy from an earlier period of skiing!) No, the whole story of inside leg action is a bit more complex—but, as usual, it helps to start out with what the foot is doing. The foot, after all, is our only direct link to the ski. What the inside leg really does in a modern turn is to "shadow" or imitate the active movement of the outside leg—without ever placing weight

on the ski! This becomes important as you carve smaller arcs. Outside leg action, we know, is a flexing/steering/pushing of the knee in the direction of the turn. Well, so is inside leg action, but with no weight.

Another interesting way of looking at it is that you are flexing and rotating the inside ski out of the way—so that the all-important, active outside ski doesn't bump into it. As we've learned, the outside ski turns through ski/snow interaction. The inside ski (the light one) is your responsibility. You must turn it with your own muscles (a minor task) so that it stays parallel with the weighted ski that is supposed to be doing all the work. In a big, smooth, long-radius turn, a gentle inward pull of the heel is sufficient to maintain this clean, narrow parallel relation. In a more active short turn, the whole inside leg comes into play, mirroring the outside leg but with no weight. Even so, the most important thing for you to concentrate on is what your foot is doing. More than anything else, we ski with our feet.

I know this entire discussion of inside leg action sounds subtle. It is. The best part, though, is how short a time it requires to start building the habit of always taking care of that light, inside ski with your inside foot and leg. You can deal with this whole business in a morning. No really advanced skier ever thinks about where the inside ski is in relation to the turning ski. It's just there, because the leg automatically keeps it from wandering, from spreading back out in a wide track. And you won't think about it either. But adjusting and readjusting your stance, adjusting the relation of your skis, is a subtle business indeed. I'd like you to continually refine and polish this skill once you get into it. That's our next topic.

Subtlety: Refining Skills, Painless Practice, Technical Games

Nothing in the world of classical ski instruction seems as onerous and negative as the idea of doing exercises. "I've got a great exercise to improve your edge control," announces the instructor, and immediately terminal boredom sets in—although generally only teenage students are up-front enough to say, "Gee, do we *have* to?" There was indeed a period—not a bright one—in ski teaching when that's about all anyone ever did in class, exercise after exercise after exercise; and the idea of just really skiing somehow got shifted onto the back burner. The pendulum fortunately swung, but it has now gone an awfully long way in the other direction. Modern instructors have embraced a "holistic" philosophy, learning while skiing down the mountain, period, and exercises be damned. Not a bad concept in itself; but as so often happens, the baby went down the drain with the bathwater. As a result, many of today's skiers have some amazing gaps in their repertoire. Luckily, there's yet another way to approach the whole business—and we can rescue part of the exercise concept, and benefit from it, without lapsing back into boredom.

It works like this: Skiing is, first and foremost, a motor activity, something physical not intellectual to be learned, practiced, and perfected in a physical way. Unlike intellectual learning, the essence of physical learning is repetition. Consider two other wonderfully developed motor activities: dancing and playing the piano. Then think of the sheer repetition, the daily practice needed to master either one. A virtuoso pianist may well warm up with a couple of hours of scales, exercises and études before starting on serious music. And even a great dancer, a Baryshnikov for example, goes to class every morning to practice the basic moves and positions in front of the barre and mirror. Thank heavens, this sort of dedication bordering on obsession isn't necessary to becoming an expert skier—but there *is* something here we can use. The whole point of practice exercises is to take one or more key moves out of context, and organize a situation where you can log a lot of repetitions in a short period of time. I want to stress that *short* period of time. Exercises have more or less disappeared from modern ski instruction because they were overdone, worked to death. All the same, we still need those intense short periods of repetition of key skills in order to refine and polish them.

So I'm going to suggest a couple of exercise-like maneuvers. But I hope you'll approach them with an untypical attitude. Think of these moves not as exercises but as technical games. An exercise is, almost by definition, boring; whereas in a game, you have at least the possibility of winning. And you will win if you increase your skills significantly. Also, I want you to practice these technical games sparingly, never for more than five minutes during an hour or two of enjoyable skiing. And finally, the best spot on the hill for such technical games is usually the least interesting for true skiing. I mean sidehills—those bothersome, slanting trails that get you from one place on the mountain to another but have no real fall line of their own. Not much fun to ski, but great for these practice games.

The best technical game of all is *sideslipping,* with all its thousand-and-one variations. Surely you know what sideslipping is, despite the fact that it's seldom taught and scarcely mentioned in ski schools nowadays. You've used it to inch down little stretches that were too steep, rocky or mean to tackle directly—relaxing your feet, releasing the edges of your skis and letting yourself slide sideways down the slope. But how and why can this simple maneuver be important? Because it contains all the elements of modern parallel turning—except turning itself. All the technical elements we've talked about in this chapter—one-footed balance (on the downhill ski) and the compensating, caretaking role of the inside leg (which in sideslipping is the uphill leg) in maintaining the skis in a close parallel relation—all are part of sideslipping, plus one other factor that I haven't stressed much yet, edge control.

There is simply no better way to tune in to the edges of your skis than sideslipping. The unsophisticated skier assumes that a ski is either edged or it isn't. Tain't necessarily so. There's a world of subtle gray between the black of strong edging and the white of a completely flat ski. And so, the first game I suggest you play is *variable speed sideslipping:* relaxing your feet and ankles just enough to barely slip sideways, then more to slip faster, then really fast, then slower again, then really slow, barely moving, then faster, etc., without ever really coming to a stop through hard edging. This should give you your first taste of the infinite subtlety of expert edge control. That sense of edging a smidgin more, or just a tad less, will of course be valuable in making your skis carve a wee bit more, or less, as you choose.

Is that all? No way. There are dozens of possible sideslipping games: For example, shifting your weight farther forward or farther backward in order to make the skis sideslip forward or backward (and incidentally discover where the neutral center point of the ski really is). Sideslipping diagonally forward while adjusting and varying the skis' angle to the hill with small rotary steering movements of the feet. Sideslipping in strange, improvised patterns and zigzags down the slope. High speed sideslips from a straight run down the fall line. Sideslips initiated and controlled with the knees (a lot of work); with the ankles (less effort); or exclusively by relaxation versus tension in your feet (easiest of all). Finally, most delicious and most practical, curved rounded sideslips: initially curving up the hill to a stop; then curving uphill only to let the ski tips again seek the fall line before curving up the hill once more (in garlandlike patterns across the hill). Especially in curved sideslips —or uphill christies, to give them a better name—you will be experimenting to find just the right combination of leg action, of weight distribution along the length of the ski, of edge, of gentle twist with the foot, needed to produce a particular curve. The combinations are infinite. As are the varieties of arcs you can draw on the snow. And this is why a few minutes sideslipping here, a few minutes there (never letting it become boring), will pay such great dividends.

One last example: Throughout this book, I've talked of the importance of the skier's feet, of communicating with and feeling the skis through your feet, of increasing your awareness of pressure and sensation in the soles. Sideslipping can give you this awareness. Try standing across the hill, motionless, edges gripping the snow, with your eyes closed. Focus on the sensations in your feet, and recognize "edging" as the sensation of weight concentrated in a line along the uphill edges of your feet. Now take that line of pressure (your weight) and redistribute it evenly along the whole sole of the foot. All of a sudden you're moving, sideslipping—and you will have gained a whole new perspective, a new feeling to associate with all too abstract expressions like "edging" and "releasing the edges." I can promise you this: the better you can sideslip, the more performance you'll coax out of your skis in each turn. It's as simple as that.

This is what I think of as indirect learning. It can never substitute for the real thing: making better turns down the mountain by riding a weighted, reverse-cambered outside ski. But sideslipping games will add immeasurably to the finesse with which you balance on that outside ski, with which you adjust pressure and edge to make it turn more, or less, for you. Do remember, please, that to pay off, sideslipping must be done with the same balance, the same weight distribution as an advanced turn. This means keeping all your weight on one ski (the downhill ski when sideslipping, the outside one of a turn); using the light foot and leg to maintain and adjust the close parallel relation of the skis. This *complimentary leg action,* in which each foot, each leg, has its own role to play, will be part of your skiing from now on. It's a universal element of modern expert technique—the only exception being in deep powder which I'll explain in chapter seven. And now you've got it.

My experience convinces me that everything I've outlined in this chapter, as important as it is, won't take you long to learn. One, maybe two days and you'll be riding the natural arc of the ski in clean, round, narrow-track turns. And loving it. What is skiing anyway but turning? A dance of curves? A magic pattern of linked arcs down a strange, snow-covered and tilted landscape? And if skiing is really turning, what could be more important than enlisting the ski it-self as an ally to make better, more effortless turns?

We've taken the first critical step toward to-tally transforming your way of skiing—learn-ing to ski on one foot to better guide the arc of the turn. Aside from that, you have only two more hurdles to cross before you enter the realm of expert skiing. So on we go.

- *The best-kept secret in modern skiing—to get the maximum turning action from your skis, stand with one hundred percent of your weight on the outside ski. The inside ski merely floats over the snow beside it.*

- *Control your speed by completing each turn in a rounded arc. In this way, how much you slow down depends only on how far around you come, not on how hard you turn. More control for less effort.*

- *To shorten the radius of the turn simply flex your outside knee forward and into the turn. The stronger this outside leg action, the tighter your ski turns.*

- *Alternating practice runs with relaxed, just for fun runs is a more effective way of building new habits than continuous practicing.*

- *Develop a sense of rhythmic vertical motion by remembering to stand back up after the flexing/steering action of each short turn.*

- *Narrow your skiing stance by pulling the light inside ski and foot (especially the heel) gently in toward the weighted outside ski.*

- *Sideslipping can be one of the best exercises/technical games for developing sophisticated parallel skills. Challenge yourself with tricky sideslipping patterns from time to time.*

3

A BOMBPROOF PARALLEL START

No More Cheating and Fudging at the Start of a Turn

Fickle friends these skis of yours, one moment trusted allies, the next traitors. . . . You've just spent one of your best days ever on skis. Was it the perfect weather? The velvet surface of mid-February packed powder? Or the fact that the gorgeous creature you met in the bar last night actually showed up at the lift this morning, and loves skiing with you? Whatever it was, everything worked. Your beautiful new round turns never felt better, your skis were really carving, leaving wonderful tracks in the snow. Why, you could have traded parkas with one of those instructors, and nobody would have known the difference—that is, until this last run. Ugh! What happened? How could you have guessed that innocuous blue trail was so steep and narrow, with so little room to maneuver? All of a sudden it was hard to turn, just plain awkward. Your feet didn't want to turn, your skis didn't want to turn, *you* didn't want to turn. You hesitated for a split second, and all was lost. Sure, you got down—but you cheated. It was the old one-two and throw them around. And now you're back on cruising terrain, known territory, and once more your skis are your friends. You heave a sigh of relief when they peel smoothly off into those beautiful arcs. But why don't they turn like that whenever you want them to, wherever you happen to be? Here on Swingsville you're parallel plus, but when the going gets tough you're still a stemmer. Your skis have started working for you, but they're not yet a part of you. What's missing?

The missing element is an unshakable parallel start. We've just spent a whole chapter talking about the arc of the turn, and I haven't offered so much as a hint on how to *start* a good turn. On purpose. For the arc of the turn—the steering, or follow-through, or completion phase as it's sometimes called—is really far more important, more basic to expert skiing than the start. But now it's time to back right up to the beginning, the initiation of the turn. Let's see if we can't polish it into an efficient, precise and foolproof parallel start.

Like so much nowadays, the parallel turn just isn't what it used to be. Once it was the be-all and end-all of ski technique for whole generations of skiers, a final goal to be achieved at all costs. Today, some self-conscious modernists in the ski world regard parallel turns as almost obsolete, near anachronisms. And they are at least partially correct in de-emphasizing the parallel-at-all-costs syndrome. Nevertheless, parallel turns will remain central to Alpine skiing for a long time to come.

It's true that the finest skiers (in particular, world-class racers, the real leaders in ski-technique evolution) have a number of non-parallel ways to start their turns: lateral stepping; divergent skating; rebounds that project them off the snow and into the next arc; et cetera. But, somehow, the parallel turn remains a kind of technical home base that good skiers always return to. In fact, the ability to pivot both skis simultaneously into a new turn, whenever and wherever one wants to, is a common denominator that sets strong skiers apart from mere hackers. Of course, when I say parallel, I'm not talking about the earlier and quite old-fashioned concept of feet-glued-together turning. (We saw what a problem that was in the previous chapter.) The modern meaning of parallel skiing is simply that both skis pivot *simultaneously* into the turn. It *is* important. And it's far easier than many skiers realize. Naturally, there's a trick to it.

The Semi-Parallel Skier: Or the Strange Case of the Disappearing Parallel Start
How about you? If you're the fairly good, yet sloppy skier I'm assuming you are, with anywhere from two to ten years of skiing experience, comfortable on green and blue slopes but stressed, nervous and awkward on blacks, you probably make what I think of as "parallel-

ish" turns. On gentle, groomed slopes it's no sweat to turn both skis together. But on steeps, and worse yet among bumps, the parallel start to your turn tends to evaporate. There's a moment of hesitation during which, solidly and safely balanced on your downhill ski, you sort of "fish out" to the side with your uphill ski, sneaking it into position for the new turn, displacing it, pointing it downhill, changing the edge. In short, sneaking it partly into the turn before you actually shift your weight onto it and go! A stem by any other name . . .

Sound familiar? Too much so, I'll bet. The case of the shaky, disappearing parallel start is so common as to be almost universal. In moments of crisis most skiers shift back to that hesitating, one-two, step/stem action. And only after guaranteeing a safe survival turn by angling the new outside-ski-to-be down the hill do they finally commit enough weight to it to launch the turn.

Psychologically, these less-than-parallel starts represent a lack of conviction and commitment. Technically, though, it's a matter of *late weight shift.* Since it's easier to change one's technique than one's state of mind, we'll focus here on the late weight shift. Or, more accurately, on developing an *early weight shift* that is, in fact, the key to a bombproof parallel initiation of the turn. Think of it this way: The only reason you are able to stem that uphill ski out toward the new turn is because it's light. As long as it's light, you can pick it up

FIG. 3.1 EARLY VS. LATE WEIGHT SHIFT. A slightly late weight shift to the outside ski invariably produces a slight stemming action (upper figure); while shifting weight to the top ski, before any turning takes place, guarantees a pure parallel start (bottom figure).

and displace it, push it out, fudge it into position aimed downhill. Now suppose that before doing anything else, you simply stepped onto that top ski (the one which will, of course, become the outside ski of the new turn). With all your weight on it, it would be impossible to move it out to the side, to stem it. And so, instinctively, unconsciously, your body would exercise its only option—turning that foot *underneath* you instead of displacing it to the side. Surprise! A pure parallel turn.

I'm not kidding, it's as simple as that (well, almost). If we consider only your *uphill* foot at the start of a turn, that foot which will soon become the *outside* foot of the new turn, then really there are only two possibilities: Either you turn that foot first, then stand on it. Or you stand on it first, then turn it. The first choice produces a stem. The second, a pure parallel start. As the weighted, outside ski turns down the hill, the inside ski *always* goes with it. But if you turn that uphill foot before weighting it, then you have to play "catch up" with the other ski.

And there's a bonus. Having weighted that new outside foot early, you'll find it almost impossible to overtwist that foot and ski, pivoting excessively and producing an awkward skid. Don't worry, the foot will indeed turn. But being weighted, it will turn more or less slowly, smoothly, appropriately. And you'll find yourself easing off into one of those long, round, carved turns we talked so much about in the last chapter (and which you've been practicing diligently, of course).

Since *early weight shift* is, I repeat, the key to a strong parallel start, I want you to go out and devote a couple of runs to it—concentrating on nothing else! Once again, retreat from your normal skiing terrain to some wide-open, not-at-all-steep cruising terrain where you can let your skis run fairly fast with confidence. And on this practice terrain, focus on shifting weight to the new ski well before you want to turn. How early? There's no hard and fast rule; but I find my students seldom take me seriously when I suggest that they shift their weight, not at the start of the turn, but truly before it. So just to stress the point, let's say: *shift your weight a yard or two before you actually want to turn.* A split second early would do just fine, but it never hurts to exaggerate when learning something new. It's like marking a full beat in music: shift . . . a . . . n . . . d . . . then turn. A nice feeling. A vital skiing habit. And each and every time it produces a pure parallel start to the turn. You'll enjoy your practice.

But that's not quite all there is to it. Early weight shift alone doesn't quite guarantee you that bombproof parallel start I promised when the terrain steepens. We'll need to add one more element. First, however, let me offer an alternative image of early weight shift that I find helps many skiers to visualize it more clearly. In the last analysis, it doesn't matter if you shift your weight *onto* the new outside foot, or *off of* the new inside foot! It's all the same. Seemingly, for about half the skiers I've worked with, the idea of lightening the downhill foot just before turning is easier to grasp and visualize—easier to feel and do. Whichever you prefer . . .

Naturally, most parallelish intermediate skiers make some sort of pole plant as they start their turn. (Whether it's an effective pole plant or not doesn't really matter here—and won't matter until we concentrate on dynamic anticipation in the next chapter.) Ideally, the pole should mark the moment when you shift weight. And it becomes very easy to use the pole plant as an effective timing mechanism when you're thinking of weight shift "in reverse" (i.e., lightening the new inside foot rather than weighting the new outside foot). You can easily lighten your *left* foot as you plant your *left* pole to trigger a *left* turn. Or lighten the *right* foot as you plant your *right* pole for a *right* turn. It fits together in a neat package.

Now when I say lighten the foot, I don't mean lifting, much less jerking that foot off the snow. Flexing that foot and ski a mere millimeter off the snow would do the trick, with much less chance of losing your balance. Indeed, I often suggest that skiers simply try to lighten the heel of that new inside foot—which keeps their weight from falling backward as the skis start to turn. And of course, the light inside heel is then ready for its next task, maintaining the inside ski in a close parallel relation to the outside (turning) ski. Once again, it all fits. Remember, it makes no difference whether you focus on shifting your weight *off*

FIG. 3.2 EARLY WEIGHT SHIFT EXAGGERATED. Although it's certainly not necessary to lift the downhill ski visibly off the snow as one shifts weight to the top ski—soon to be the outside ski of the new turn—it's easier to form a clear mental image of early weight shift when one sees the inside ski raise off the snow a split second before the turn starts. That is what we view here.

the downhill ski, or *onto* the uphill ski, a split second before turning. Six of one, half a dozen of the other. Whichever works for you. But do it early!

Now let's take early weight shift and make it into a much stronger technique. On steeper slopes, early weight shift alone won't do the trick. You have to move onto that top ski, and then let your *whole body* continue to move forward and down the hill into your intended turn. Believe me, on super-steep slopes this is scary indeed. (But of course, you shouldn't be on super-steep slopes yet.) What I've just described is the physical equivalent of committing yourself to the new turn. I could describe it variously as tipping, or leaning, or tilting downhill toward the new turn; as letting your body "fall" forward and down the hill; as projecting the body into the new turn; as moving into the turn, body and soul. You get the picture, I'm sure. For some time, ski coaches and ski technicians have called this important and subtle move *crossover,* because the skier's body crosses over the skis and tilts to the inside of the next turn.

Why crossover anyway, and why is it progressively more important the steeper the slope? More than anything else, the body's downhill tilt serves to flatten the skis momentarily on the snow, rolling them off their old edges, which allows them to pivot smoothly into the fall line. The steeper the slope, the more the edges will be biting, and the more we must tilt downhill to flatten them. (For a graphic picture of this tricky phenomenon, see fig. 3.3.)

It works. Although at first, tilting downhill feels a bit like sticking your head in the lion's mouth, your skis will peel off into the turn twice as smoothly. You may have the unsettling feeling that if the turn doesn't happen, you'll fall right over on your head. Correct. But somehow the turn always does happen. And you quickly learn to live with that delicious insecurity.

How to practice this crossover, this commitment of the body into the new turn? Here are a few tricks, any or all of which should be helpful. First, still on fairly flat easy slopes, try to become conscious of what part of your foot you're standing on. After an early weight shift to the top foot, let the pressure roll across that foot to build up on the fleshy pad just behind the big toe. This tells you that your body is indeed moving forward and to the inside of the next turn. As your body moves, your foot is actually rolling the ski over from its old edge; first flattening it on the snow, which facilitates the initial pivoting; then, as pressure builds on the inside edge of the foot, rolling the ski onto the new inside edge of the turn. It will not only help your crossover but also develop far more ski/snow sensitivity if you learn to tune in to these changing pressures in the soles of your feet.

Foot pressure is a subtle matter—and so are weight shift and crossover. Or at least, they should be! No one needs to see a big,

FIG. 3.3 CROSSOVER. Crossover is the second factor in a bombproof parallel start, present in virtually all turns, but progressively more important as the slope steepens. Here we see the skier's body incline smoothly toward the center of the new turn, facilitating edge change and a smooth turn initiation.

lurching weight shift at the start of your turn. It can be all but invisible, just as the fact that you're riding the outside ski around its arc is not visually obvious. So, rather than lurch from ski to ski, you shift precisely, deftly, lightly. And crossover too should be just as smooth, just as subtle. The body doesn't pitch across the skis; its movement should be smooth, progressive, inevitable.

Another thing you can do to facilitate this crossover, this commitment to the new turn, is to put a bit of weight on your pole instead of just symbolically tapping the snow with it. That's right, lean on it—just a little. The pole you're planting is on the downhill side so it can give you some momentary support in your slow-motion fall or tilt to the inside of your new turn. This support from the pole becomes much greater, even critical, the steeper the slope.

And here are a couple of technical games you can play with, which really give you the feeling—an exaggerated but interesting feeling—of the body's crossover down the hill. One is called "the thousand steps" and is nothing more nor less than walking (step, step, step, step, etc.) around the arc of an easy turn. You can start by just traversing across the slope with this step-step-step action (like walking in place on your sliding skis). You'll quickly discover that you can never get the skis to start "walking" around the corner, into a downhill turn, until you yourself lean over downhill. Once you do so, the skis seem to follow, step-stepping right around. (Try this, too, on a gentle slope.)

Once you've felt the downhill-tilting action of the body in the thousand steps, try something harder—an exaggerated one-ski turn. Like this: Traverse diagonally across a moderate slope for twenty or thirty feet, entirely on your uphill ski. (Lift the downhill ski well above the snow just to make sure you don't cheat.) After this short, radically one-footed traverse, simply turn downhill! (On that same foot, of course.) The only way you'll be able to do so, will be to let your body really tilt down the hill —just as though you were going to fall over downhill on your nose. A kind of test, both of your one-footed balance and of your gumption, your ability to force yourself to lean downhill toward the intended turn. But this game you're playing is so extreme, so exaggerated, that you'll learn an immense amount from it. Returning to the normal understated start to a normal parallel turn, you'll have a much better feeling for the subtle commitment of your body into the new direction.

Summing up then, the total secret of the modern parallel start to the turn is *early weight shift* followed by a *commitment of the body toward the new turn.* This whole bit with the body is a more or less natural happening that really takes care of itself in most circumstances. Only on steep slopes does it need conscious attention, or a lot of practice.

So now you know the whole story of the bombproof parallel start. Early weight shift is going to require the most concentration. And the sooner you make a habit out of early weight shift the better. For you'll be using this kind of parallel start everywhere, in the most diverse circumstances. (Perhaps I should add, for the sake of accuracy, that early weight shift works everywhere *except* in deep powder, which in skiing is the exception that proves all rules!)

Wrapping up loose ends, I should mention that early weight shift is the exact opposite of that old "Hup!" (or up-unweighting) that so many skiers learned as an essential part of starting a parallel turn. Unweighting was indeed necessary to free those earlier, stiffer skis from the grip of the snow in order to turn them. No longer! On groomed, packed slopes modern skis turn almost too easily. What we're really doing with early weight shift is *pre-weighting* the new outside ski, even before the turn starts, so that it will bend into reverse camber as soon as possible, peel slowly off into a clean arc, and turn the way it was designed to. Easy does it. Which brings us to our next topic.

Eager-Beaver Initiations and Panic Parallel

Aside from the on-again, off-again, ho-hum, parallelish start I've described above, there are a couple of other hangups and problems with the parallel start that could easily block any further progress, and slam the door shut on our vision of expert skiing. Chief among these is the wild and woolly, parallel-at-all-costs death pivot! This particular vice, an overtwisted, overinitiated and generally equal-weighted parallel pivoting of the skis into the new turn, is most typical of young, athletic and self-taught skiers. Such skiers don't learn skiing step by step in ski-school classes, and being impatient to get on with upper-lever skiing they simply imitate what they see (or *think* they see) good skiers doing—turning both skis at once. Well and good; but as we've learned, there's a lot to advanced skiing that isn't so obviously visible. And so these eager-beaver skiers seldom pick up on the importance of weight shift, of riding the outside ski. Their turns are typically overinitiated and under-steered: excessively violent parallel twisting at the start, then a kind of half-hearted uncontrolled skid to finish.

If you are one of these skiers, you surely know it. Perhaps you've already started to feel a major change in your style while you worked on riding the outside ski in long arcs as I suggested in the last chapter. But till now you've actually been so proud of your ability to twist both skis together into any turn that you haven't even considered that there might be another way of starting turns. It's time to slow down. Not only does excessive twisting put your skis at too great an angle across your direction of travel, producing far more skid than you see in experts' turns; but also with such violence, you've used up your whole range of motion early on, and you have nothing left to guide the ski in the second half of the turn. Net result: no outside leg action and no finish to the turn. Which means that in bumps and on steeper slopes you'll be constantly struggling with loss of balance and lack of positive speed control from one turn to the next.

So we're going to cut our initiation, the start of the turn, down to the bare minimum we can get away with. You'll have to give up twisting both feet equally and concentrate on early weight shift. Stepping on the new outside ski early, and then—and only then—twisting it in the new direction, is quite sufficient. As the weighted outside ski peels off into the turn, the light inside ski naturally accompanies it—and you won't have lost any of the parallel quality of your turn, only its violence.

Once again, it's fiendishly hard to concentrate on early weight shift and a slow, smooth entry into the turn if you're on a very difficult slope. At the risk of repeating myself, let me stress once more that no one can build new habits in a challenging and stressful situation. Panic parallel is one result—and it won't get you anywhere. So back off a notch, down to easier cruising slopes, and pay some dues. Start forging the habit of early weight shift, coupled with riding the outside ski around the whole arc. Learn to savor and enjoy the smooth, carving style of skiing that results from this. A good ski turn, like a glass of great wine, should be good to the last drop—stretch it out, savor it, make it last. Don't rush through it as though you were gulping down a glass of soda.

Parallel Problems out of the Past: The Compulsive Stem Habit

At the other end of the spectrum are those skiers who perhaps took too many ski lessons, too many years ago. And who, although basically strong, steady skiers, have been fighting a nagging, compulsive stem-step-shuffle at the start of every turn for decades now. Although the analysis of the problem (late weight shift) and the correction (early weight shift) are exactly the same for such skiers, it's just not that easy to change.

"Habit is habit," said Mark Twain, "and not to be flung out the window by any man, but coaxed downstairs a step at a time." And so it is with this sort of skier. One afternoon's serious, high-minded concentration on early weight shift, even if it achieves some results on easy, open slopes, is still not going to eliminate ten or more years of a cheating little stem-push at the start of every turn. But don't despair! There's hope for you, too—even though Twain's metaphor about coaxing the habit downstairs is not quite accurate.

Motor habits, in a sports context like skiing or tennis, are seldom isolated gestures or movements. Instead, like this perennial stem, they are part of a sequence, a chain, a complex of moves that occur together, in the same order, time and again. In this case, the sequence is the entire turn. And such sequences are generally triggered by one typical opening move; more often than not, in skiing, the gesture of hand and arm that readies the pole for planting in the snow. In the case of deeply ingrained movement patterns, it's often a waste of time to try to change one element in the whole sequence. The only real chance to break the negative habit is to build up an altogether new sequence of movements, *triggered by a new initial step.*

That is why, if you're one of those skiers who has lived with such a stem for too long a time, I don't think you'll have much luck trying to substitute early weight shift for the late weight shift of your stem. What you need is a whole new way of triggering the turning process, a new start to replace that same old arm/ hand/pole action that triggers your stem. And you'll find such a new way to launch turns in the next chapter. It's called a preturn, and should give you a whole new habit pattern to build on. So, patience! Don't, by all means, give up on early weight shift. It remains the sine qua non of an easy, efficient parallel start. But don't expect miracles either. If your bad habits go way, way back, then you'll just have to go on to chapter four and the mysteries of dynamic anticipation more or less on blind faith.

We're coming to the last of the three all-important technical elements that form the basis of expert skiing. And as you're about to see, this last one ties it all together.

- *Late weight shift (i.e., turning the foot first, then standing on it) is the usual cause of a nagging stem at the start of the turn—especially in tough terrain.*

- *Early weight shift (i.e., getting onto that uphill foot before the turn) is almost always sufficient to produce a pure parallel initiation with no fudging or cheating.*

- *As slopes steepen, become aware of crossover—the natural tilt or lean of the body across the skis and down the hill. This commitment of the body into the turn facilitates an easy change of edges and, together with early weight shift, guarantees a pure parallel start.*

- *A slow, progressive parallel start via early weight shift is almost always preferable to a violent, overenergetic muscular pivoting of both skis. Slow it down and give the ski a chance to work for you.*

- *If a stem habit is deeply ingrained—a compulsive habit from years back—it may be quite difficult to replace it with early weight shift. Patience! The preturn described in the next chapter should do the trick.*

THE BIG BREAKTHROUGH

Linking Turns with Dynamic Anticipation

9:00 A.M. A crisp early morning lift ride. Slanting sunlight in bold beams stripes the slopes beneath you, setting afire the crystal surface of a three-inch overnight dusting of powder. A white-furred ermine runs for cover in the trees beside the piste. The only sounds are the gentle squeak of the chairlift shivs and a light wind rustling through the pine tops. . . . Suddenly two skiers burst out of the woods; almost unintentionally figure-eighting each other down the narrow steep trail beneath your chair; slipping, snaking and bobbing over a set of bumps where the trail steepens to a wall; relaxing past the bumps into a series of long, smooth, drawn-out arcs; disappearing from sight as fast as they came. It takes your breath away, that kind of skiing. And you can't help asking yourself: What is it? What's the difference between such skiers and, well, ordinary mortals? All that's left of this fleeting vision are the two tracks they left upon the light dusting of new snow. A clue? Perhaps. You turn in your chair, fascinated, staring back down at those two sinuous lines while the lift carries

you on up, up, into another day of glorious skiing. What is it these brilliant skiers have scribbled so clearly across the snow?

The message is clear when you know how to read it. And that's what this chapter is all about. The question is so important that I'd better rephrase it before trying to suggest an answer. What, exactly, is it that constitutes expert skiing? (Aside, that is, from obvious details we've already talked about like riding the arc of the ski, or crisp, clean parallel starts.) The answer is simple once you see it: *Experts are always turning!* They seldom use the traverse/turn/traverse/turn pattern so typical of average skiers. They prefer to link one arc to the next and then the next in a kind of seamless transition that appears so smooth, so natural, so inevitable, that it's hard to separate the end of one turn from the beginning of the next. That, of course, is part of the trick; for in expert skiing, the end of one turn really *is* the start of the next. This trick, or technique, I call *dynamic anticipation.* And it produces a way of skiing that is not only exceedingly graceful, but also physically easier and more efficient than a style built on individual turns separated by traverses. The best skiers *always* link their turns into continuous, ribbonlike sequences, and this produces the rhythmic, flowing, dancing quality of expert skiing. That was the message left on the snow in the early morning scene at the start of this chapter. And this style is what you're about to learn.

As you might suspect, there's more to it than simply wanting to turn continuously, or trying to eliminate all traverses by a continuous, ongoing effort to keep turning. Dynamic anticipation is a real technique, a complex and integrated movement pattern, which can be learned, practiced and mastered. In one sense it is *the* technique of advanced skiing. Because the main difference between even very strong upper-intermediates and truly expert skiers is simply that the experts use dynamic anticipation and the others don't. And since this movement pattern is so important—and so tricky—I'm going to break our discussion of anticipation into three parts: understanding it; learning it; and finally, applying it to almost every aspect of your skiing.

The Still Center of the Turning Skier: Understanding Anticipation

Anticipation is a mighty peculiar word to describe a ski technique, but it's been around for some time and I suspect we're stuck with it. In the ski world, anticipation most often conjures up a picture of a skier whose upper body is facing squarely downhill—an oversimplified and inaccurate view. The anticipation I'm talking about is emphatically *not* a simple position, nor even one simple movement. It's an entire integrated pattern of movement, of action and reaction, that expert skiers use to link their turns. This is why I prefer to call it *dynamic anticipation* to avoid confusion with the all-too-static misconception of anticipation as a mere upper-body position.

*FIG. 4.1 LINKING TWO ARCS WITH DYNAMIC
ANTICIPATION. A general view of the way expert skiers
typically use the end of one turn to launch the next without a
pause. The skis appear to "unwind" or "re-turn" toward the fall
line beneath the skier's body; and the start of such turns feels
virtually effortless. Linking turns with dynamic anticipation is
the master skill for expert skiing—a kind of watershed that
separates average skiers from experts.*

Dynamic anticipation is a pattern of movement characterized by the following factors: Upper body independence—the skier's trunk no longer following the skis, right and left, around each turn. Active leg actions (and reactions)—the skier's legs and skis turning out from under the body, only to re-turn back to neutral beneath it. And perhaps most important, the build-up and release of muscular tension between the passive upper body and the active legs—the storing up of twist or rotational energy at the end of one turn that can then be released to start the next turn. Does this description ring a bell? Sure it does. The skiers you admire all ski like this.

Skiers using anticipation appear to have highly mobile, active legs and skis that turn freely, back and forth, beneath a calm, almost motionless upper body. This can be seen most clearly when the skier links a series of short-radius turns. The body appears to be following a straight line, an invisible wire, down the slope while all the side to side, right and left action occurs below the hips. One has the impression, watching such skiers, of a body separated into two halves, linked by a free-swiveling universal joint somewhere around the hips. Indeed, "upper/lower body separation" has become a synonym for anticipation.

This general effect—upper body passive, quiet and motionless, while legs and feet do the job down below—is less visible but still present when truly advanced skiers link turns of any size, even long-radius swoopers. But more is going on here than just keeping the upper body quiet while you ski. In actual fact, the legs do most of their work near the end of each turn's arc (that flexing/pressing leg action we talked about in chapter two), building up a kind of last-minute tension between upper and lower body—winding the skis up against the stable mass of the trunk so that when this tension is released, the skis seem to *untwist,* to straighten out, to turn back down the hill into the next arc almost on their own. Almost without effort.

This effortless initiation is the true promise, the real importance of the anticipated style. Average skiers make their greatest muscular effort at the start of each turn, getting things to happen. Typically, the expert puts more effort (and attention) into a strong finish for the preceding turn, and then virtually relaxes into the new turn, *allowing* the skis to pivot back down the hill rather than forcing them to do so. This is the intermediate's classic parallel turn turned inside out. And this relaxed effortless start puts the skier in a neutral, balanced position entering the new arc, so that the entire range of leg motion can be applied to guiding the curve with finesse. A free start to every turn. Sounds too good to be true—but it works.

How precisely does it work? Like this: The skier's upper body (trunk, hips, arms, head) is about twice as heavy as the legs or lower body; and so it has twice as much inertia. This means that if the muscular connections between upper and lower body are relaxed, the upper body will turn much more slowly than the legs and skis. Of course, legs, feet and skis are more actively involved in turning anyway; the body is only a passenger. So what typically happens at the end of an anticipated turn is that the legs and skis, being lighter, have come farther around the corner, more across the fall line, than the skier's upper body has. The upper body *seems* to be facing momentarily downhill, across the skis, anticipating the coming turn. (Hence the name "anticipation" given to this style by French coach, Georges Joubert, years ago—a label that's stuck despite endless misinterpretations.) At the end of one turn then, the anticipated body is ready to move across the skis, downhill toward the new turn, while the legs and skis that have "wound themselves up" beneath the trunk, now "unwind" into the new arc. . . .

The winding and unwinding image is a great one to keep in mind as we try to form a clear mental picture of how dynamic anticipation works and why it's so important. This image implies that the actual work has somehow *already been done* before the moment of truth when the new turn starts. Seen from outside, such turns seem to start effortlessly, by themselves. From the skier's point of view, it feels as if feet and skis are merely *straightening back out* where they belong, back into their normal position beneath the body—and this return to normal starts the new turn.

What I've just described, legs winding up

and unwinding, is a far cry from the usual corny concept of anticipation as "skiing with the body facing downhill." But it's easy to see how this misinterpretation came about. (How many ski-school classes have been told to ski with "shoulders turned downhill" or with their "bellybutton always facing the lodge"?) Now while it's true that such a position might well make it easier to start the next turn (the upper body being, in a sense, already halfway around the corner, already in the fall line), treating anticipation only as an upper-body position results in a one-dimensional caricature of true dynamic anticipation. All the real action of dynamic anticipation takes place *below the hips.* The steering/guiding action of the legs brings one momentarily, for the briefest instant, into a position where upper body faces downhill across the skis. But then, just as swiftly, legs and body move back into alignment, skis swinging smoothly back beneath the trunk. An active and rhythmic working of skis, feet and legs beneath the skier's still center, the unmoving upper body: out of the fall line, then relaxing back into the fall line, twisting out of the fall line again, and back. . . . A pendulum of activity beneath a quiet body, that's dynamic anticipation.

And what is it that makes all this not only possible, but actually easy? Another secret. The skier must "disconnect" the trunk from the legs by relaxing those muscular connections that, when tense, tend to lock us into rigid one-piece units. In particular, to achieve the real upper/lower body separation of anticipated skiing *you must relax the small of your back.* Muscle tension in this critical area condemns the skier's body to swing from side to side along with the skis. Not that tension anywhere else in the body is good—merely that a relaxed lower back is an *essential* ingredient of the anticipated style.

To finish off this overview of dynamic anticipation, I'm going to talk you through the anticipated transition between two turns. What you do. And what you feel. These are not instructions—too much happens all at once. This is only one last set of images to familiarize you with what anticipation is all about. Afterward, we can get on with the more important business of actually learning, and mastering, the anticipated style. (I discovered long ago in skiing that understanding something and doing it are not, alas, synonymous.)

Let's say you're finishing a turn to the left, riding the outside ski in a round arc that you control by flexing, pressing and steering your right, outside leg. As you complete the turn and pressure builds underfoot, you find yourself facing somewhat downhill across your skis. Your relaxed upper body simply hasn't turned as far out of the fall line as your skis have. And at the same time, you're reaching forward, down the hill, with the tip of your right pole. Now! Simultaneously you plant your pole, partially supporting yourself on it, and from your flexed position you rise up onto your other foot—your top or left foot, the outside foot of the coming turn. Not just "up," but actually *letting your body move up, forward and down the hill at once,* moving across the skis, the same way you were facing at the end of that left-hand turn.

And what happens? As your body moves across the skis, they flatten and pivot beneath you, following you into the new arc. And now, of course, you're already standing on your left (new outside) foot, ready to flex that leg just as fast or as slowly as you want to guide this new arc. You're off and turning; but the beauty of it is that the skis seemed to come around on their own. They've unwound beneath you. And because your strong pole plant anchored your body in its downhill-facing direction, all the unwinding took place down at the ski level. Just what you wanted: another effortless turn!

In such turns you feel yourself in a real state of grace. You become a privileged passenger, floating above your skis. You offer simple signals, suggestions, and your skis obey. You—the real you, your awareness, your body, your hips that are actually your center of gravity—you keep moving smoothly forward down the hill. While your skis do their thing beneath you, you feel like the still center of a turning world.

Naturally, when broken down step by step, the linking of even two turns sounds devilishly complicated. It is—when analyzed. Worse yet, in ski learning analysis often leads to paralysis. So we're going to pursue a simplified, even roundabout path to acquire this pattern of dynamic anticipation. That's what we'll tackle next. But at least we now share a common picture of what dynamic anticipation really is: a total pattern of movement linking two turns, not just a position in which the trunk faces downhill. It's the glue that links individual turns into smooth, effortless, dashing combinations—endless S's down the mountain. It's a hell of a way to ski.

Preturns, Practice and Patience: Learning Anticipation

Patience, more than anything else, is what you're going to need in order to make dynamic anticipation a part of your skiing style. Not infinite patience, but a lot of it. Because in my experience it takes most skiers at this level about a week—and never less than three days —to accomplish such a major change in their skiing patterns. It's worth it. I wasn't kidding when I called this chapter "The Big Breakthrough." Everything so far has led you to the anticipated style; everything from now on depends on it. Learning to use dynamic anticipation truly constitutes the watershed in a skier's development—his or her passport into expert skiing.

So when I talk about being patient, about being willing to spend up to a week of your skiing life concentrating on anticipation, it's a small price. Not much to ask, really, considering the payoff. You won't struggle for days on end without making any gains; progress will be continuous and inevitable. But I'm talking about more than just trying a new move and getting it right once or twice. I suggest that it will probably take you about a week to truly *absorb* anticipation into your way of skiing, to make it a solid habit, to integrate it as an almost subconscious movement pattern—anticipation on autopilot! Of course, this time/ patience factor explains why so few recreational skiers ever really get the hang of skiing with anticipation. If you've ever taken any advanced ski classes, your instructors certainly skied this way. They may even have talked to you about it, tried to demonstrate it. But at the end of the lesson you found it didn't stick. Now you know why. Such complex, integrated motor habits, like Rome, aren't built in a day. So now, armed with that necessary extra measure of patience, let's begin.

Our approach will be twofold. On the one hand, we're going to play around with the spontaneous linking of turns. A holistic approach, just doing it, in the hope of achieving a crude approximation of anticipation that we can then refine. On the other hand, we'll take the moment of truth right out of context—that critical anticipated transition between one turn and the next—and practice the daylights out of it in the form of a wonderful technical game, the *preturn.* But first, as a kind of warm-up, how about a little static (in place) practice to see what anticipation feels like.

Stand up tall and loose (on your skis, or on the floor at home) and notice how your whole body—eyes, chin, chest, stomach, hips, knees, feet—seems lined up, pointing more or less straight ahead. This is your normal or "home-base" anatomical position. Now, relaxing and flexing a bit, turn your whole upper body to look 90 degrees sideways, right or left. Then straighten back up. Repeat this movement a couple of times to each side. What you're experiencing is a grossly simplified version of the winding up and unwinding that characterizes dynamic anticipation—although, on the slope, it won't be your body moving but rather the legs twisting and untwisting beneath it. In this sideways twisting you will feel a kind of muscle tension or pulling in your side, as body and legs reach the point of maximum opposition. This tension is part of what makes the skis untwist back beneath the body.

Now let's do more. Remember, I said that a *relaxed lower back* was the real secret of effective anticipation. To feel what I mean, try this experiment: Still standing up, place one fist in the small or hollow of your back, and then tighten your back muscles to push hard against this hand—that's right, until it starts to hurt! Now, after holding this uncomfortable position for, say, a count of three, release all the tension. Whew! . . . What happens? Your stance, your posture changes dramatically. Your hips drop and your fanny which was sticking out now seems to tuck forward. The small of your back is no longer so "hollow"— a sure sign of excess tension. At the same time, your shoulder blades relax, your shoulders round themselves forward, and your arms loosen as well. This is the ideal stance of the anticipated skier. By exaggerating lower back tension, then releasing it, you can really feel the difference. And now, with a relaxed lower back, you have effectively released all the muscular connections that tend to weld trunk and legs into a rigid, one-piece unit. To prove this, repeat that sideways twisting movement a couple of times, alternately with a tight and a relaxed lower back. What a difference! Relaxing those lower back muscles seems to create a flexible, rubbery hinge in the region of your waist and hips. With this posture, upper/lower body separation is not only possible, it's easy. So let's stand like this from now on.

Back to the slopes now, to start building the habit of anticipation. Your first task (assignment, challenge or game) will seem deceptively easy. Simply try to eliminate any straight lines, any traverses, between turns. I don't just mean 20 or 30 feet of traversing; even two or three feet, even a split second of traversing between turns, is too long. Why? Because in those few feet any natural anticipation, or tension between upper and lower body that may have developed in the previous turn, will dissipate and you're back to square one.

It's a question of timing. And the timing cues I want you to pay special attention to are all in the soles of your feet. As you finish a turn, any turn, pressure builds up under your outside, support foot. When you sense that for a particular turn this pressure is at a maximum, shift to your other foot. That fast! No waiting, no fussing about or getting ready—just get on the new foot! Often, since you'll be in a some-what flexed position, the easiest way to shift weight is by extending or straightening up on the other foot. But at this point it's less impor-tant how you get there than getting there *fast.* Of course, this is the same old *early weight shift* we've talked about so much—only here we're focusing on early weight shift from the end of a preceding curve, not from a traverse. Okay?

You will not immediately succeed in elimi-nating all the gaps between your turns. But this idea is so general, so useful, that you can play with it everywhere, on every run. Nor is it just a question of trying to ski in a tight rhythm, trying to link short turns (short swing) straight down the fall line. Any size turns, from tiny to giant, can be linked together without a hint of a pause. As usual, moderate, medium-to-long-radius turns will give you a little more time to sense what's happening, to tune in to the pres-sure clues in your feet, to concentrate on mov-ing that all-important weight shift from some vaguely future moment to the here and now, to the exact finish of each turn. It's almost as though you were trying to blur the distinction between the end of one turn and the start of the next. There is actually only a split second that divides them—the instant you pass from one foot to the other. And you can mark this crucial instant with your pole plant, a helpful gesture that often eliminates hesitation. Late pole plant equals late weight shift. But however you do it, the space between two turns has got to go! Hesitation here, just as much as a tight lower back, can be a kiss of death for the anticipated style.

But unfortunately, just bringing your turns closer together doesn't do the whole trick. If, as I've assumed, most of you have many seasons of rather ho-hum skiing behind you, then it's unrealistic to rely on the sort of natural anticipation that so often appears when kids and very young skiers start closely linking their turns. Rather than hoping for it to happen, we'll *make* it happen with the most powerful, and most neglected, technical game in skiing: the *preturn.*

A preturn is nothing more than the tail end of any good turn, taken out of context and practiced by itself in the form of an uphill christy. But the preturn is a very special kind of uphill turn, one in which the turning skis come farther around, farther up the hill than the passive body that is left anticipating or facing somewhat across the skis (pole ready to trigger a possible new curve down the hill). The preturn brings us to that critical, magical moment at the end of one curve when tension between upper and lower body is at a maximum, when the body is primed, coiled, twisted against itself in readiness for a new turn.

Luckily, *the preturn can be practiced without the downhill turn that would normally follow.* That's why it's so important. Because at

FIG. 4.2 A PRETURN. The end of an advanced turn taken out of context. The skis turn up the hill more than the skier's body does, producing a sort of "windup" or tension between upper and lower body—upper/lower body separation—that can be used to facilitate the start of a new turn. The preturn is probably the most important technical game, or exercise, for expert skiing.

this level of dynamic anticipation, the holistic approach of just "doing it" breaks down. Linking two turns with anticipation looks effortless, and in a sense it is. But it involves a tremendous amount of coordination—quiet upper body, pole preparation, pole plant, early weight shift with crossover, followed by new outside leg action: too much! Believe me, by taking the key elements out of context (thereby avoiding the actual crisis of trying to start a good turn) and by repeating these key elements with awareness, feeling and concentration—that is, by playing with the preturn— you have a far better chance of absorbing the whole integrated pattern.

The situation is analogous to the problem white-water kayakers face when trying to learn an "Eskimo roll" that will right them after capsizing in rough water. The Eskimo roll, too, is a complex maneuver involving coordinated movements of legs, hips, arms, shoulders and paddle—all to be executed while one is upside down and backwards underwater! No one could possibly get it right in the middle of a boiling rapids and so the kayaker must retreat to the relative calm of a swimming pool to practice this critical skill. In just the same way, we are going to retreat momentarily into the relative calm of an uphill christy (turning uphill from a traverse to a stop) in order to integrate this whole pattern of active leg action beneath a motionless, relaxed upper body.

Head down across the hill, picking some sort of target like a particular tree, lift tower or mountain peak that you can continue to face while your legs guide the skis in an uphill arc beneath you. Start the preturn itself by sinking while you load the downhill ski; and continue that flexing leg action to guide the skis uphill to a stop. Not a simple sideways twist, please, but a real round arc up the hill. Okay? Duck soup. Legs and skis turn up, you don't. And you come to a stop facing somewhat across your skis, still lined up with that original target you chose. Now, after a couple of successes, let's make the game harder. Concentrate on your hands and poles. Hands in the classical balancing position, about hip-high and spread in front of your body. As you sink and steer the skis uphill into what is quickly becoming a preturn, just tilt your downhill wrist forward, advancing the point of that pole. Not only is it ready to plant, but it tends to plant itself as you steer your preturn to a stop.

Now—even though our goals involve *continuous* motion, into and then out of anticipation, quite the opposite of any frozen positions —I still want you to take a moment to check out your position as your preturn comes to a stop: legs flexed, downhill ski loaded, uphill ski light, body twisted or "broken" slightly at the waist/hips so that your whole trunk is facing down across the skis (its original direction), arms wide, downhill pole planted not right beside the skis but well below them. In this position, you feel like a crouched tiger about to spring across your skis and down the hill. Well, I exaggerate a bit, but not much . . .

Once you can do this uphill preturn to a stop on either side, what next? Let's keep making the game harder (and more realistic, I might add). Now, instead of skiing your preturn to a stop, come only partway around. Then, as pressure begins to build on your downhill (outside) foot, plant your pole and support yourself on it for an instant while quickly stepping up onto your top foot. What happens? That ski will start to turn back beneath you, seemingly on its own, until it returns to the direction of your original downward traverse, the direction your body is still following. (Caveat: if your weight shift isn't total, it won't work and all you'll get is an awkward semi-stem of the top ski.) Aha! A partial curve up the hill, and a partial unwinding back. You've just experienced firsthand what I've been talking about for pages.

But don't rush it. This whole business depends on your ability to guide the skis in a turn independently from your body, right out from under your body that continues to float merrily along in its own direction. (Actually, even if your lower back is very relaxed, your trunk will still turn a bit, but much less than the skis, producing our momentary position of anticipation.) So the very first step of my suggested sequence—skiing toward a target while pivoting the legs and skis uphill away from it—is critical. It's okay to literally "hold" your body facing downhill at first; with a little more practice, a little more relaxation, it will simply stay that way by itself.

How much is a little practice? You can feel your first successes with this preturn game in twenty minutes or half an hour. But it will take days to make it a habit. No, not days of just repeating preturns to a stop across the hill, thank god. That would be too dull for anyone, however dedicated. Instead, I'll ask you to alternate, say, ten minutes of preturn practice across the hill (on sidehill trails preferably, and always to both sides) with two or three long, relaxing, fun runs. But don't ski any terribly challenging slopes, right at the very limit of your ability, during this period. Survival skiing at this stage only produces excess stiffness and tension that will cancel out most of your anticipation. Stick with comfortable cruising slopes for a while as you get into preturning, and your patience will be richly rewarded.

But preturns alone, you're thinking, lack a certain excitement. Of course they do. So on we go to the next phase. Our goal is to use the preturn as a kind of springboard to launch effortless downhill turns. The real thing. We've already found that a pole plant and weight shift before the preturn comes to a stop will cause the ski tips to tilt back down the hill to their original traverse line. And we've left some nice curved tracks across the hill this way: curve up, pole/shift, curve back, then curve up again, etc. Now we go just a bit further. With a bit more speed than you've been using so far, start a preturn up the hill, and before you slow down too much I want you not only to plant and shift but also to let your body move right on forward across your skis (the full crossover). Presto, your skis not only tilt back downhill a bit, they arc right around into a full downhill turn. A very important kind of downhill turn because it was a *reaction* to the preturn, not an action in itself. A happening, a coming-back-to-center from the anticipated position, an effortless free start that leaves you perfectly balanced on your outside ski, ready to guide the new arc. Almost for the first time you will understand why real experts never look as though they're working to turn their skis. They aren't.

A few more points, pointers and a warning: One very common error can rob you of all the reaction, the effect you're supposed to get from your preturn. If you hesitate, even for a second, for a couple of feet or a couple of meters, between preturn and turn, then all is lost. Well, not all. You'll still get around the corner. But you will have dissipated all the tension between upper and lower body that helps pull the skis back down the hill. Timing is critical; which is why I've asked you to plant your pole and trigger a reaction turn well before the preturn is over, in the midst of the action. Consider some of the other sports where windup and release mechanisms (or action/reaction mechanisms) are important. A baseball pitcher, for example, never pauses at the end of his windup, or all the force of the pitch that follows would be dissipated. A tennis serve is another good example. You can't raise your racket into position, then toss the ball up, and expect to deliver a powerful serve. Back stroke and fore stroke must be one smooth, continuous movement. Yet almost always my students start out making beautiful preturns—and then hesitating between preturn and turn. Forewarned is forearmed: don't fritter away all you've gained with such untimely pauses.

Your first success feels great: what a turn! But one hot anticipated turn from a preturn doesn't cut it. We need hundreds to make this style of turning a habit. So your practice pattern will now consist of three types of skiing. First, I want you to keep on breaking things up with relaxed fun runs. Second, periodically throughout the day, whenever you're on a wide slope or sidehill, I want you to quickly knock off several sets of preturns across the hill. Do some to a complete stop, as a kind of self-check to see if your preturn is really taking you into that anticipated position. And do some only partially, that is to say, not stopping but shifting weight and pivoting back to your traverse line across the hill. Third and most important, practice our new way of turning. From time to time devote an entire run to launching individual turns from preturns. In this case you will obviously traverse between turns, in order to take a moment, concentrate and set yourself up for the next preturn. Not to worry. Our aim here isn't yet the total fluidity of anticipated skiing, but simply a feeling of moving into and out of anticipation (via the preturn) at the start of each turn, an awareness of the skis' "windup" and "re-turn" to the fall line.

When using your preturn to set up and

launch a complete downhill turn, try to ski a little faster than usual and take a steeper line down the hill toward your intended turn. Why? Because, although the preturn offers some powerful advantages, it also robs you of speed as it turns back up the hill. Lose too much speed or angle and you won't make it back around the corner! The sequence of feelings you experience in a preturn/turn begins with speed. You swoop down the hill, free and fast. Preturning, you create resistance and braking; pressure builds underfoot. Launching the new turn with pole plant, weight shift and cross-over, you feel this pressure and resistance disappear, *allowing* the skis to move back to where they belong—following the original line of your momentum down the hill into the new turn. The key feelings: pressure, then release.

I haven't mentioned it yet, but it should be clear that this pattern of preparing for a downhill turn via an uphill preturn is the ultimate solution for the compulsive stemmer I mentioned in the last chapter. If you've been using a mini-stem for years to fudge your way into turns, the preturn should eliminate it. Since the initial movement in the sequence (sinking and steering the skis uphill) is quite different from what you habitually do to turn, it's not likely to trigger old motor patterns. You'll be building a new parallel habit from scratch, without interference from your old habits. At last . . .

But something, I know, is bothering you. Preturns may be a super-technical game, they may teach us a lot, but you don't see real experts using a preturn (a little uphill hook) before each turn. I've said it myself: they turn *continuously*. So why should you spend so much time trying to master this preturn? Good question. If you do see expert skiers make a preturn, it will typically lead only to the first turn of a series. For once a series of turns is underway, *the end of each turn serves as a preturn to launch the next*. Remember, "preturn" is just the name we give to the finish phase of an advanced turn with anticipation when we take it out of context and use it separately. The only reason we do so is to simplify the situation and focus our attention more clearly on the movements of dynamic anticipation. Although practicing preturns is an extremely important part of learning dynamic anticipation, the separate, isolated preturns will tend to disappear as we put it all together. At first, though, you can't do too many of them.

Finally, one last reminder about the rhythm, the sequence and alternation of effort and relaxation when skiing with dynamic anticipation. The pattern is: work first (preturn), then relax and enjoy the result (the new turn). Work, then relax. Flex and steer, then rise and float. *Make* your skis turn up, then *let* them turn back down, *Action;* then *reaction.* All turns involving dynamic anticipation (and the variety is endless) are, in a sense, "reaction turns." Their almost effortless quality is the result of what's already happened. This goes a long way toward explaining the stress I've laid on a positive finish to your turns (chapter two). In the last analysis, a well-finished turn gives you the start of the next one, gratis! And this is true whether the turns be rapid-fire short swings, long arcing cruisers, or something in between. Which brings us to a whole new point. So far I haven't even suggested what size preturns and turns to practice, assuming that you would stick to something you felt comfortable with and avoid extremes. But now that preturn practice has started to give you a feel for skiing with anticipation, we need to explore a wider range of options.

Going with the Flow:
Using Anticipation Everywhere

Different slopes, pitches and personalities all call for different turns. And surely matching your moves to the mountain is part of the expert's art. To find out how versatile our preturn/anticipation pattern is, let's now make a wide variety of preturns. Try some short quickies with rapid sinking and strong leg action that bring you to a stop in a meter or two. Then some long fifty-footers, arcing gradually around almost without moving. They're all preturns though: upper body relaxed, passive, floating above the hips while the legs do their thing. And they all end with a pole plant.

What do you notice? First, that the shorter and quicker your preturn, the more anticipation you get from it. In a sudden quick preturn from a steep angle down the slope, you'll wind up facing straight down, 90 degrees of anticipation across your skis that have turned clear across the hill. In a long gradual preturn, you may wind up facing just a wee bit across your skis, not quite lined up with your ski tips but almost—let's say, only a few degrees of anticipation. Now we aren't sports scientists, and the last thing we want to do is go around measuring degrees of anticipation; but nonetheless, something important is happening here.

Remember that the unwinding effect I've been talking about only brings the skis back until they're lined up, normally, with your body. So if you have very little anticipation, the skis only come back a little way—just the sort of gentle, small pivoting that you want to start a long-radius turn where the skis need only turn bit by bit, not all at once. Conversely, if you have maximum anticipation (facing clear across your skis), then your skis will pivot right around, wham, into the fall line—just what you need for starting a snappy short turn. Curious but true: *a given-size preturn produces just the right amount of anticipation to start another turn of the same size.* Short quick preturns give you the anticipation you need for a short quick turn. The reaction from a long-radius preturn will be a long-radius downhill turn, and so forth. Now you know how to create an effortless advanced turn of any size. Just guide your preturn through the same sized arc.

But are all these anticipated turns really effortless? I've tossed around a lot of expressions like "unwind" and "untwist" that imply the skis simply snap back beneath the body on their own. It generally feels that way, but I confess, the reality is more complex. The rapid twisting action of the legs in a short preturn (or when finishing a short turn) may indeed stretch the opposite set of rotating muscles so far, and so fast, that the stretch reflex comes into play, actually snapping the legs back, a good example of real automatic unwinding or uncoiling. But in most cases, and especially after medium and long arcs where you finish with only moderate anticipation, the skier's legs really do work to bring the skis back in line with the body. However, they work much less than they normally would. The muscles involved have been prestretched (by the preturn) so they tend to contract more efficiently. Above all, since the heavy body is literally "preturned" down the hill, and since the legs and skis are relatively so light, the force required to turn them is minor. So minor, indeed, that the feeling is always one of effortless, spontaneous unwinding—whether the legs are working or not. The principle is always the same. The anticipation gained in a *preturn* (or at the end of a previous turn) provokes and facilitates a *re-turn* of the skis down the hill. Just as I promised, this gives a free start to your turns.

You should definitely be feeling this incomparable ease by now—if "by now" implies at least two or three days of playing around with anticipation and preturns. Once you start to develop the confidence that a good preturn really does set you up for a free start to the next turn, you should pursue the same feeling, the same result, without making clearly defined, separate preturns. It's simple. After a preturn to launch the first turn in each series, let the end of that turn serve as your preturn to start the next one, and so on. . . . It won't be letter-perfect at first. That free anticipated start tends to come and go. But you'll definitely feel it when it works. You should probably alternate between carefully set up individual preturn-into-turn experiments, and simply trying to keep the preturn effect working in a series of linked turns, all the way down the slope.

As this style of skiing becomes easier, try to integrate it with the shape of the terrain you're skiing on. As you know, no ski piste is uniformly smooth. There are always high and low spots, rolls and hollows, natural curves and shapes as well as skier-made moguls and gullies. Try to end your preturns on the tops of large natural rolls, which produces a delightful extra feeling of lightness as the skis arc back around the other side. Likewise with big and rounded moguls; but don't, please, take your new anticipation skills into serious, mean moguls too quickly—even though dynamic anticipation is an absolute prerequisite for bump skiing as we'll see in chapter five. For all too many perennial intermediates, bumps have been a crisis for years; and the stiffness and tension produced by such crises can wipe out your anticipation habit before it's really formed. Sticking to moderate blue slopes for

FIG. 4.3 LINKING LONG-RADIUS TURNS WITH ANTICIPATION.
*One long arc blends smoothly into the next. The degree of
anticipation is much less pronounced than in short turns, just
barely enough to get the job done.*

FIG. 4.4 LINKING SHORT-RADIUS TURNS WITH ANTICIPATION. *Here the apparent degree of anticipation is very pronounced. The upper body appears to face constantly downhill as the legs turn from side to side beneath it. Yet this "body down the hill" image is more of a happening than a conscious effort. Active legs, a passive trunk and a relaxed lower back are the secrets of this extreme dynamic anticipation.*

a while is part of that patience I advised you to practice. But even so, ski the big, rounded, natural shapes as though they were macro bumps, guiding one arc always to the crest, the high point, of such a shape, and letting the reaction turn take you on around the other side . . .

After a few days' practice, as you start more and more of your turns with preturns, or with the preturn effect, I hope you'll develop your own personal sense of what dynamic anticipation is all about. I find it hard to pin down with words because, as I mentioned earlier, it's neither a single movement nor a single position. More than anything else, dynamic anticipation is a way of moving between two turns! It's not so much that your body faces across your skis. What counts is that *the body moves across the skis,* flows forward into the new turn (and the skis, of course, always come with you). There is not a single frozen moment in the dynamic anticipation used by real experts. It's what defines them, in fact: going with the flow.

When you find that this flow—this movement of the anticipated body into the new arc while the legs turn and re-turn beneath you— starts to feel comfortable, natural, even inevitable, you may as well buy a bottle of champagne to celebrate. You will have made the biggest single breakthrough in a skier's career, and turned the classic intermediate parallel christy inside out, so that now it starts by itself. All the various worlds of expert skiing begin opening up.

But can you really do it? Especially on your own, after reading this chapter? I'm an optimist. I think most skiers can. But clearly the toughest part of the task will be applying yourself to the program I've sketched out. When I'm lucky enough to ski with interested and eager students for a whole week, it always works! But there I'm pulling the strings. I can keep slipping highly focused practice periods into days filled with exciting skiing. My students thus log hundreds of preturns without really realizing it; and I always make sure there's no danger of boredom or burnout.

It's a bit different for a do-it-yourself ski learner. One thing though, you're not completely on your own. The slopes are loaded with living examples: the good, the bad and the ugly (and yes, the beautiful). Now that you understand what dynamic anticipation is and how it works, you can use each chairlift ride to gather images, sort things out, reinforce your perceptions, simply by watching the skiers below. Even so, it's still a do-it-yourself project. You have to believe that, this time, you're really going to transform your style of skiing— and give it your best. Don't be fanatical. Relax and just ski for fun too; but keep coming back to anticipation and preturns, five or six times every day, maybe only for ten minutes at a time, perhaps for fifteen or twenty. But keep after it. Hundreds of good preturns, and the reaction turns launched from those preturns, should be enough to change everything in the course of one week's skiing.

One reason it's such a do-it-yourself project

is that you're not likely to find a ski-school class or program where you can spend the needed time, day after day, mastering dynamic anticipation. Sadly, the whole technical concept of anticipation has been somewhat downgraded in today's teaching scene. The old, clichéd version of static anticipation ("turn your body down the hill") still surfaces in mogul skiing lessons—but it's mostly lip service paid to an incompletely grasped concept. Yet I can understand why anticipation is underplayed. It's awfully hard to teach. Too hard for most ski-school programs. And instructors and students alike only get frustrated if they work on something that "doesn't take." The real fault of course is lack of time and commitment. I hope by this time I've convinced you to invest enough of both to get the job done.

You now know what dynamic anticipation is and also its importance. It won't be long before you feel it, live it, breathe it, ski it, consistently. Hang in there. Real freedom on skis is only a preturn—excuse me, a couple of hundred preturns—away!

- *Dynamic anticipation is the principle that lets skiers effortlessly link their turns, using the end of one turn to start the next.*

- *It is not a "position" but rather a style of skiing in which the legs move actively*

*beneath a quiet, relaxed upper body—
building up rotary tension at the end of
one arc that can then be released to start
the new turn.*

- *The secret of this "upper/lower body
separation" is to ski with a relaxed lower
back; and the best way to practice and
learn dynamic anticipation is via preturns
—uphill arcs in which the legs and skis
are turned out from beneath the skier's
body.*

- *As you begin to ski with dynamic
anticipation, concentrate on eliminating
any hesitation or "dead spot" between
two turns. The end of one turn literally
becomes the beginning of the next.*

THE MULTIPLE WORLDS
OF EXPERT SKIING

PART
TWO

5

MOGUL MADNESS

*Bashing, Boogiing and Dancing
Down the Bumps*

You're still waiting for those butterflies
in your stomach to stop fluttering, settle
down and maybe doze off. You've been
standing here at the lip of this incredible
mogul field—is it Exhibition at Squaw,
Pallavicini at A-Basin, or Prima at Vail?
Could be any number of steeply tilted,
pimpled and pockmarked playing fields
for the demented. You've been standing
here for five minutes and already it
seems an eternity. The bumps below you
are big, big and mean, choppy and steep,
more like fangs actually, or tank traps . . .
and not at all inviting. But they must be
so to all these other skiers, creatures
from another planet maybe, who
smoothly slip by you over the lip and
disappear down the fall line, snaking
through those bumps as though, well, as
though they belonged there—legs
oscillating like rubber pistons, bodies
motionless, poles deftly picking out a line
where all you can see is the possibility of
linked disasters. And you know they're
smiling. Yesterday you did so well on
those friendly blue bumps that you
thought, Why not? Maybe today. You

**were wrong. You don't belong up here
and you know it.**

Happens all the time, doesn't it? The average skier, after a couple of such mistakes, concludes that bump skiing isn't his or her thing. "I'm into cruising," they tell themselves and retire from this unequal combat as gracefully as possible. But of course, bump skiing doesn't have to be a battle, much less a losing one. You can probably guess what I'm going to say next. Expert skiers make bumps look easy because they ski them in an easy way. The frustrated hacker, over his head in the middle of a tough bump run, is not simply psyched-out; actually his problems are technical more than mental. Skiers who have trouble with bumps are almost always using inappropriate, counterproductive techniques, awkward false movement patterns that no one could get away with—not even the hottest skiers on the hill. Well, we're about to change that.

Bump skiing is terribly important for anyone who wants to become a true expert. For one thing, bumps are everywhere. Bumps are ubiquitous, ever-present features on all steep slopes at modern ski areas; and they sprout again, hydralike, as fast as the area's fleet of snow cats can mow them down. In an attempt to reassure nervous students, I often point out that the only reason bumps exist is because high spots on the slope help skiers to start their turns; so skiing bumps ought to be easier than skiing on a groomed slope. But I know it's not true. One bump, perhaps; but hundreds, tightly packed down the hill, no way. The passage of each skier, scraping more snow out of the trough, makes the bump that much steeper, more abrupt, harder. And so mogul fields become more difficult day by day, until sometimes even the hottest bumpers wish the snow cats would flatten them for a fresh start. Bump skiing is simply the biggest challenge the modern skier faces, every day at every ski area. But I can promise you: if you've learned to link turns with anticipation, you can not only learn to ski bumps well, you can learn to love them. (The word *mogul,* by the way, is simply a skier's term of obscure origin for the simpler *bump.*)

I've already claimed that the problems people experience in skiing bumps are more technical than psychological. Still, anything we can't handle physically will also psych us out; so the two factors, technique and state of mind, are certainly related. Our main task, though, will be to replace a set of awkward "survival" moves with a more efficient movement pattern. To help you understand just what has to be replaced, let me sketch out the all too typical, awkward mogul turn, the full catalogue of disaster.

Unskilled skiers approach the crest of a bump as a crisis to be lived through and gotten out of the way as fast as possible. For this reason, somewhere up near the top of the bump they always overpivot their skis, swinging them all the way around past the fall line in the blink of an eye. The bump, by providing a natural pivot point that lightens the skis, unfortunately aids this folly. And, presto, with the skier now facing back in the new direction, the turn is over almost before it started . . . but the crisis is only beginning. Generally after this overpivoted start, the skier will slam back into the side of the same bump, a little farther down; and the ski tips will help chip out one of those awful vertical cliff walls that mar the downhill side of so many bumps. Even failing that, the overpivoted start has put the skier's body across the hill (losing any anticipation) and used up the whole range of leg motion—there's nothing left to steer the turn to a safe finish! Worse yet, this violent start creates tension and stiffness in the legs that overedges the skis. Such strongly edged skis, unfortunately, can only accelerate. And if they don't shoot right out from under the unbalanced skier, will lead him off across the slope, faster than he'd like, slamming into the next bump to the side, and the next, and the next. . . . Sounds bad? It is. To change all this we'll first figure out the secrets of a really good mogul turn; then we'll focus on stringing such turns together into great bump runs; and last, we'll take a look at some extreme cases, some of the mind-boggling, body-bending radical shapes of moguls at their most challenging.

Making Your Peace with Bumps: Coping with the Modern Mogul

Where do we start? Why not with the shape of the bump itself. And with that perennial question: Where do I turn? Not all bumps are alike but they all seem to have a few features in common. Viewed from above, the top of the bump is more of a rounded ridge or crest than a single high spot. On either side are two steeply cut flanks, usually of hard, scraped snow. Farther out to each side are two more or less rounded gullies or troughs where the snow is often softer, as this is where all the loose snow scraped from the sides of the bump winds up. The gullies lead clear down around the mogul, to a kind of smooth shelf separating it from the next mogul down the hill. All too often the very bottom of the bump is a kind of wall or mini-cliff that has been hacked out by ski tips at the end of panicky, overpivoted turns. Crafty skiers avoid these mini-cliffs like the plague.

The bad news: there is no one perfect place to turn on a bump. The good news, however: there is a loosely defined path (capable of many variations) that expert bump skiers follow over and around most bumps. Note carefully, over *and* around, because the optimum path is neither all on the crest (skiing *over* the bump) nor all in the gully (skiing *around* the bump) but a bit of both. This optimum line will certainly elude you for a while on the hardest bumps, for one thing, it will seem too fast until your braking reactions become truly quick and sophisticated. But I still want to give you a clear picture of an optimum bump turn, before we devote our attention to the series of steps that will actually give you the confidence to use it.

The classic bump turn begins somewhere up on the crest of the mogul, just as the skier's feet are crossing its hump. You already realize, I'm sure, the importance of starting things at this key moment when tips and tails are momentarily suspended in air, and the only ski/snow contact is underfoot. It's almost too easy, which is one reason we see so much overpivoting. In fact, the skis should pivot *slowly* downward, crossing only a part of that steep, scraped flank, to arrive somewhere in the middle of the gully still pointing down the fall line. Many gullies are only a foot or two wide, so if our two-meter skis have pivoted clear to the horizontal by the time they reach the gully, they just won't fit. Finally, the turn should end with the skis following the gully on around, completing an actual arc *beneath* the mogul, on that smooth shelf that typically separates two bumps. It's only down there that one really has enough room to complete the turn.

Of course, there are variations and even exceptions to what I've just described, but this is the pattern of turning that will eventually change those unfriendly, desperate-looking, cliff-sided bumps into playgrounds for you. I'm talking about a rounded turn, not a sudden pivot. (S-shapes instead of Z's, although actually the strong finish beneath the bump gives this turn more of a J-shape, or hook at the end.) It's a matter of using the best shapes on the bump and avoiding the worst of it. Three key elements are involved in this turn: the anticipated start, the tricky balance, and speed control. Let's look at each in detail.

The relaxed, unhurried start depends one hundred percent on anticipation. Maximum anticipation with the body facing squarely down the fall line, so that the re-turn of the skis beneath the body will bring them all the way down, into the gully, without the need of any extra twisting or violence on your part. A perfect passive start to the turn, which saves you both energy and the full potential for active leg action to be used at the finish. To guarantee this position of maximum anticipation, a simple but effective trick: plant your pole *much farther down the hill* than normally, really stretching down there. (This is only the first of many times I'm going to talk about your poles in connection with bump skiing. They are far more critical than you might imagine.) Planting your pole way down below your feet not only insures that your upper body's facing downhill, it also gives you something solid to lean on as you tilt downhill to let your skis turn. I've talked about a slow initiation, but actually it's not *that* slow. Your skis will turn rapidly enough. I'm just asking that you not add any extra leg rotation to their natural unwinding from anticipation. And just because you find yourself in the unfamiliar world of bumps,

FIG. 5.1 THE CLASSIC BUMP TURN. *Gradual pivoting from an anticipated position on the crest of the bump; a round arc in the gully beside the bump, and a strong finish beneath the bump itself. No extreme positions, no violence.*

don't go and forget to *shift weight to the top ski!*

Now let's consider balance. The angle of the snow you're skiing on changes radically from one moment to the next. The shelf on top of the bump is much flatter than the average angle of the slope. The scraped away sides of the bump are much steeper than the slope itself. So every few feet, the bump skier must pass from flat to steep to flat and back to steep again. A tricky bit of balance adjustment indeed. Especially since as your skis drop over the crest onto the steep flank of the bump, they speed up drastically. Most skiers get left behind, on their heels, at this point in the turn, and wind up struggling for balance when they should be steering the end of their arc. To prevent the skis from running out from under you, you must tilt your body forward at the start of the turn—not to "get forward" but just in order to keep up, and stay balanced over your feet. This is not an easy task because tilting downhill as you go over the cliff-like lip of many bumps is rather like pitching head first off a tall building. Another hand/arm/pole trick should do the job for you:

As you start to turn, don't only lean on that downhill pole you've just planted, but also *advance the tip of your other, outside pole quickly down the hill toward the next bump,* the next turn. This is mostly a wrist action; your hands, spread and forward as usual, scarcely move in bumps. But by advancing the new pole with your wrist, by reaching straight down the hill with it, you will automatically bring your body forward over your skis. It's typical of the very best bump skiers that by the time their skis have pivoted into the fall line, the point and basket of the outside pole are always advanced, always ahead of the hand, projecting down the hill like an antenna. This is a must, not an option. By flicking the new pole forward down the hill, you are not only rebalancing over your skis but also preparing for the next turn—both physically (the pole, by moving straight down the hill and not swinging around, helps hold your upper body motionless, in anticipation) and mentally (you look down the pole at your next turn, as if sighting a target).

The final most critical part of an efficient bump turn is speed control. This is the missing element for so many skiers who go faster and faster from turn to turn, simply because their turns are all initiation, no follow-through and finish. The secret of speed control in bumps is twofold: a strong finish below the bump, and skis that sideslip rather than carve on an edge. Strange that I should say this after having stressed the unique carving abilities of modern skis. The reason is simple: The shape of the turn we follow around the bump is already there, inscribed in the snow in front of us in the rounded banked track of the bump's gully. Any sliding ski will follow this natural arc in the snow, so real carving is superfluous. Worse yet, on the steeply angled side of the bump any edging becomes a lot of edging, and strongly edged skis are more likely to accelerate out from under the skier. Skiing bumps with relaxed, loose ankles and feet allows your skis to sideslip around the curved shape of the bump with just as much precision as a carved turn on the flat—but the sideslipping skis are gently scraping away at the snow, slowing down all the while. Serious braking, of course, comes from a strong finish to the turn. As I've already pointed out, the only place where there's really enough room to bring the skis all the way around—without bashing into the bump itself—is on the relatively smooth shelf below the bump, or sometimes on the upcoming shoulder of the next bump down the hill. To use this space means delaying the leg action of a strong finish until you've slipped *past* the bump, and the coast is clear. Then finish the turn with a strong, quick sinking/steering action, all the while moving that outside pole straight down the hill toward that next bump. And here we close the circle, because that strong leg action at the finish gives us the dynamic anticipation needed to start the next turn. That rounded uphill hook beneath the bump (on a long bump the track stretches out to become more J-shaped than round) works just like a preturn, bringing us right to the crest of the next bump as it slows us down and winds up the legs against the body. A neat package.

But a scary one if you try to ski like this in the biggest, hardest bumps—at least without enough preparation. Learning to ski bumps is a phased effort. The rule of thumb is: learn to ski medium bumps well by practicing in small ones; learn big bumps by practicing in medium bumps, and so on. The rapid-fire pace of bump skiing makes it impossible to concentrate on technique and line when you're skiing at or near your limit. Back off until you find a bump field that looks easy by comparison and there—with a relaxed mind—work on slowing down the start, and delaying the strong finish of your turns. The problem of course is the sense of extra acceleration that comes from a slower pivoting into the fall line, and the slight hesitation in finishing your turn. The fact that you have more room to finish, down below the bump, will amply compensate for any extra speed you pick up. The net result is that you can ski bumps much slower. You can even bring yourself to a complete stop on the lip of that next bump, since the "pivot-point effect" on a bump's crest makes it possible to turn with no forward speed at all. And that's not a bad learning game to play: slow pivot, slide, sink and steer to a complete full stop; slow pivot again, etc. But I repeat, your only chance is to build this pattern (slow anticipated start/ delayed strong finish) one step at a time, notching up the difficulty as the pattern grows stronger.

It may have occurred to you that once again we've taken the average turn and turned it inside out. Instead of twisting hard at the start, then relaxing, we're now relaxing into the fall line, then twisting out. The anticipated style at its most useful, but now adapted to the shape and the demands of the bump. It's the same old/new story: the bump turn begins with release of pressure, ends with the build-up of pressure. And psychologically, you'll find, the pressure's off. Naturally, I haven't told you everything about individual bump turns, only the basics so far. But before talking about refinements, let's address the task of linking dozens of these turns into long, elegant bump runs.

Variations on a Theme: Putting Together Great Bump Runs

Individual turns don't add up to great runs. What counts is the flow, the smoothness, the grace, the dash with which you move from each turn into the next. For this reason, as usual, most of our attention will focus on the end of the turn; not just on the *how* of ending one turn and starting the next, but even more on the *where*. At West Point, military cadets study both tactics and strategy, the small-scale movements and the big picture. In skiing we face something similar, a balance between *technique* and *strategy*. Technique, of course, is the *how*. Strategy the *where, when* and *why* of our sport. Strategy in bump skiing means choosing a good line through a confusing white labyrinth. Just how does one do this?

The goal in mogul skiing is continuous, linked turns, more or less down the fall line. To the perfect bump skier, one mogul is as good as the next, and there's no need to choose better shaped bumps or avoid badly shaped ones. But during your bump skiing apprenticeship, such choice is everything. Once launched into a good bump run, your option is limited to whatever you happen to find just below the mogul you're turning on. Therefore, your success or failure often depends on that first bump—so for heaven's sake pick a good one! To see if a bump is inviting or ugly, I always look at the exit: the terrain I'm going to run into as I complete my turn down below the bump itself. Is there enough room to complete the turn? Does one of those sharp mini-cliffs extend all the way across the gully? Does the bump end in a smooth slanting shelf that will lead me nicely to the next crest—or does the gully become one of those godawful V-shaped slots with no room to turn at all? Most bumps have friendly exits, but some are a lot friendlier than others, so in sizing up the next bump always look past the lip to what awaits you below.

Of course, you'll want to choose your first bump partly by the next few bumps it leads you to. There's a myth going round about how expert skiers are always looking four or five turns down the hill, plotting their strategy many moves ahead like chess champions. I certainly don't, and I don't know anyone else who does, either. Looking two turns ahead—at the next one after the one I'm skiing—is plenty. But what, precisely, am I looking for? Depending on the speed I want to ski at, and the shapes of the next rank of bumps down the hill, I am making up my mind whether to take the short or the long exit from each bump. This is the key factor in picking a line down any mogul field, so I'd better explain the concept of the two different exits from a bump.

If you were standing on the crest of a bump with a bucket of water in your hands and hurled it into the gully, where would it go? It would swirl down, following the gully around the bump, and then flow out the bottom, sloshing around the next funnel-shaped gully, and so on straight down the hill. Since bumps don't line up exactly, one above the other, but are slightly offset down a hill, there is generally a fast-exit gully waiting at the bottom of each bump. This is the *short exit* I mentioned above. Skiers who chose this exit let their skis follow the "watercourse line" I've just described; they wind up skiing mostly in the gullies, seldom bringing their skis around very far out of the fall line—and they usually ski quite fast. The *long exit* involves steering your skis farther around, past that first-exit gully and even slightly uphill over the crest of the next bump to the side. (Figure 5.2 furnishes a graphic picture of these two exit lines.) Prolonging the curve, sweeping under the bump you've just turned on and up the flank of the next bump below and to the side, slows you down a lot—even in spots where there seems to be no room to finish the turn right below your bump. The turn is longer, rounder, and you have more time to get it right. You also use the long exit for changing your line, moving

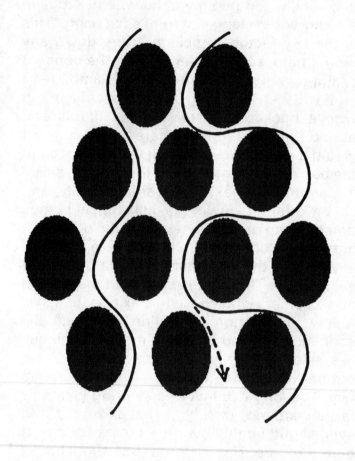

FIG. 5.2 FAST AND SLOW LINES IN BUMPS. *The most important choice in picking your line is the exit you choose beneath the bump. Turning downhill again into the first gully you see is the fast exit (left vertical line). The slow exit (right line) involves passing that first gully, rounding your turn slightly uphill over the shoulder of the next bump to the side, and only then turning back downhill—a longer line with more time and space for braking. The two lines, fast and slow, are shown separately but, of course, they can be mixed together at will (dotted line).*

it over one set of bumps to the right, or left.

Which exit are you going to use? Both, of course. Short of simply traversing across the mogul field looking for a better place to be— something to avoid at all costs, since traverses create balance problems as you hit bumps, rob you of anticipation, and generally rein- force any hesitation to plunge downhill—short of traversing, your choice of long or short exits from each bump is about the only mechanism you have for altering your line down a mogul field. You'll find it quite adequate. Naturally, a field of easy, rolling, moderate-sized bumps is the place to get familiar with these two pos- sibilities for straightening, or rounding out your line. The watercourse way, a series of short exits, is incredibly graceful, slippery-feel- ing and elegant. It can be skied with almost pure leg/foot relaxation and no real effort. But unfortunately, it just doesn't slow you down. It is the path of choice in low-angle easy bumps. As the bumps steepen, you'll have to throw in a progressively greater percentage of *long* fin- ished turns, arcing out of the fall line and up over the next bump to your right or left. Both the long and short lines are important parts of the bump skier's repertoire.

But whatever your line, the crux of it all is to keep going, to keep linking your turns down the hill. Time after time, inexperienced bump skiers seem to do everything just right, make a beautiful turn and arrive right where they ought to be for the next perfect turn—only to miss it. Oops! They weren't ready. Most of you

FIG. 5.3 OUTSIDE HAND AND POLE ACTION IN BUMPS. A critical factor! Extend your new outside pole ahead of you down the hill with quick wrist action—as soon as your skis start around the bump. This helps you stay anticipated, and above all, prepares you (psychologically as well as physically) for the next bump and the next turn.

know just what I'm talking about. The answer, the glue that connects turn after turn, end to end, into beautiful runs, is effective hand/pole action. I've already touched on this, but it bears repeating. When you're actually linking your turns smoothly down through the bumps, you will feel as though you are walking downhill on your poles! Often, in very tight bumps, the new pole hits the snow before the other pole comes out of it. So redouble your concentration on advancing the outside pole as soon as your skis begin to pivot downhill. Don't wait until the last minute as you finish your turn to get that pole ready. As a rule of thumb, make sure the basket and point of your pole are ahead of your hand by the time your skis reach the fall line. (Remember, this is a bumper's trick and has nothing to do with cruising and long-radius turns.) And while I'm on the subject of poles: be careful not to let the pole you plant drag your arm (and weight) back by hanging on to it too long at the start of your turn. After planting the pole, and supporting yourself on it for a second as the skis start to pivot, just keep moving your hand forward down the slope. Fundamentally, the hands and arms don't really change their basic position in bump skiing (forward and spread); all the action, and there's plenty, involves the wrist and pole.

Does it surprise you that I'm putting such stress on pole action? The best one-sentence summary of modern technique is: *Ski with your feet, balance with your hands.* And as we've seen, the high art of bump skiing is one of balance and timing, exactly the areas where effective hand/wrist/pole action can make a difference. I want you to take this very seriously. Quick, precise pole action is just as essential for expert bump skiing as an effortless anticipated start to the turn. So essential, in fact, that if you're having a bad day in the bumps, usually concentrating on reaching down the hill with that outside pole is enough to get you back in the groove, to reinforce your anticipation, eliminate hesitation, improve your timing. Even slow-speed bump skiing involves making a turn every second (!), so time —and the subjective sense of having enough of it to deal with the coming bump—is critical. Rapid pole action will give you that time.

It's probably obvious but I should add that you'll need another kind of time too—practice time to build the habit, and the confidence, to link turn after turn after turn, right down the middle of even moderate mogul fields. Reduce the task to manageable proportions by breaking your run into sections. Tell yourself: Okay, six turns without stopping. Not bad! Now ten. Now a dozen. Then pull out, skiing the long-exit line to a stop. Smile, congratulate yourself, take a deep breath; and if you feel like it, up the ante before dropping into the fall line once more. At first you'll want to plan your route, long line or short etc., down the first three or four bumps before you push off. Later you'll just take the bumps as they come and adapt. If you're reasonably cunning at distinguishing good practice bumps from those that offer too extreme a challenge, you'll soon be linking turns from the top of the slope to the bottom. Remember, good bump skiing doesn't have to be fast, but it's always continuous.

What else? *Absorption* is another factor that relates more to the flow of the whole run than to individual turns. By absorption I mean the shock-absorbing action of the skier's legs that can, in effect, smooth out moguled terrain. Mogul fields are a succession of hollows and humps, highs and lows. And skiing through them at a reasonable clip, one encounters both compression shocks and moments of excessive lightness, where partially airborne skis can no longer work with the snow—or would encounter such problems if one didn't use leg action to "smooth out" the bumps. Skiing bumps at slow speeds, or working on timing and technique one turn at a time —dropping from a full-stop anticipated position on top of one bump to a full stop at the lip of the next—there's simply no excess pressure to absorb. But once your bump skiing takes on a certain flow you begin to notice that each bump pushes back, compresses you. And with bigger bumps or higher speeds, it can get pretty rough. Nevertheless, the solution is simpler than ski teachers and technicians have ever let on. (Unpronounceable imported terms like *avalement* and *reploiement,* and the hair-splitting concepts they represent, have muddied these waters to the max.) And here's how it works:

Watching gifted bump skiers flowing down a mogul field at respectable speeds, you notice that what strikes you first is the constant, pistonlike up and down movement of the legs —a folding and unfolding synchronized with the high points and hollows of the terrain that allows the body to travel undisturbed. This shock-absorbing action of the legs reminds you of slow-motion television commercials for automobile suspensions. Fortunately, the skier is responsible for only half this action: the unfolding, or downward extension of the legs to fill up the hollow spots, troughs and gullies of the bumps. If your legs (thighs) are fairly relaxed and already slightly flexed, then your feet and skis will automatically be pushed up beneath you, compressed or flexed, whenever you hit the shoulder or lip of a bump with enough force. If it happens, fine; if not, don't worry—flexing would have been superfluous. All you have to concentrate on is extending your legs to fill the gaps—and even more important, to ensure that once again your shock absorbers will be fully extended so that they can absorb the next compression.

Once the basics of your bump skiing technique start to feel comfortable and established—anticipated start, rounded line and choice of exit below the bump, plus quick pole action to link turns—then you can focus your attention completely on this reextension of the legs. It's a constant effort to "get tall" again, as the continued compression of the bumps tries to squash you shorter and shorter.

I'm not talking about the radical compression experienced by certain bump skiers who seem to take delight in choosing the most brutal line possible, smashing full tilt into the most abrupt lips and bumps they can find. Even following your optimum rounded line *around* the end of the bump, you will still experience a certain compression as you finish your turn against the shoulder of the next bump. The active leg action that guides this finish, sinking and steering, is itself a kind of compression. Typically, you'll finish one turn in an anticipated *and flexed* position right before the lip of the next bump. Just delay the reextension a split second until your feet and skis have pivoted over that lip, and *voilà,* you'll be in perfect sync with the terrain. Instead of the body rising up as you reextend the legs, you will be extending feet and skis downward toward the bottom of the trough or gully. Nifty!

One more sidelight on this vertical shock-absorbing action of the legs to smooth out bumpy terrain: such leg play (passive relaxed folding caused by the bumps, plus your own active reextension) demands real flexibility and looseness. Such extreme looseness in turn depends on a nearly *vertical back.* Another bumper's secret! We already learned in chapter four that a relaxed lower back is an essential ingredient of effective anticipation; but this is something more. By bending forward at the waist, you tighten a lot of the muscular connections from lower back, across the buttocks, and into the legs—directly limiting

FIG. 5.4 ABSORPTION/EXTENSION AT HIGHER SPEEDS. An upward folding of the knees and legs is the natural way to absorb the shocks of higher speeds—or more abruptly shaped moguls. But the critical, active factor is the reextension of the legs on the other side of the bump to prepare for absorbing the next shock once again.

how deeply you can flex your legs. Maximum possible leg flexion is only available with a vertical back. Just look at the best bump skiers at your own ski area. The very best of them, the ones who appear to have rubber legs, ski with bolt-upright backs. You can too, and your legs will be twice as flexible for it. The only danger with this bump skier's posture is that in moments of extreme flexion/absorption you may find yourself too far back on your heels (especially since our boots don't allow very much ankle bend). Avoid this backward loss of balance through the simple expedient of always keeping your hands spread and forward, always reaching downhill with the new pole.

With this much technique, you've already changed from a bump hater to a pretty good bump skier, but you're not yet master of the meanest moguls. Shall I let the cat out of the bag? With appropriate technique you can become a pretty good bump skier in a short time; but it takes years plus a certain talent and temperament to become a great bump skier. Be that as it may, you'll still arrive at the point where you'll be tempted to trade the security of basic bumps for a taste of really radical ones, the toughest the mountain has to offer. Here too I've got a bag of tricks for you.

Radical Bumps: Secrets of the Full-Tilt, Fall-Line Boogie

The time has come to take you far beyond the basics of good bump skiing into a flashier, more challenging dimension altogether. Skiing bumps well is one thing; but skiing them with flash, dash and panache is another. In addition to possessing the personality for it, and the sense of security and comfort that only comes after toting up lots of mileage in bumps, you're also going to need some additional skills: first, a kind of ultra-rapid pivoting for lightning quick changes of direction between very small, sharp bumps where classic turns are too slow; second, a way of dealing or at least coexisting with impossibly shaped bumps (cliffs and no-exit V-slots) that have a habit of suddenly appearing like roadblocks in the middle of your line.

One of the characteristics of a great bump skier is having fast, indeed super-quick, feet. When the bumps are big, rounded and inviting, top skiers spend a lot of time following the watercourse line, flowing smoothly around each bump on the rounded, banked walls of the gullies. But when the bumps get small and tight, such skiers are able to rev up their turning rhythm to two or three quick pivots a second, which gives them the option to suddenly change line, pivoting back to seize a new option before the last turn has really gotten under way. *Option* is the operative word here, because our basic approach still holds—the average bump turn, if there is such an animal, should have a relaxed, almost slowed-down start. But super-quick pivots can and will get you out of many a jam. They're easy if you use what I call super-anticipation or, more to the point, lower-leg swiveling.

You'll remember that in the previous chapter I described the anticipated style as a "pendulum of activity beneath a quiet body." Super-anticipation is typified by a pendulum of activity *beneath the knees!* That's right, only the lower leg (shins, calves, feet) appears to move, in a pendulumlike swiveling beneath a body whose thighs now seem just as still and motionless as the hips and trunk. The first place to experience what I'm talking about is while sitting in the chairlift. With thighs supported by the seat, let your feet swing back and forth beneath you. The skis don't exactly turn, but do appear to slant back and forth at an angle from one side to another—a sort of mini-turn.

Now try to re-create the same feeling on a very flat smooth slope (a groomed catwalk works fine). In a slightly seated position, relax your feet and ankles to permit maximum side-slipping, and try to "blur" your feet and skis back and forth under you in a kind of mini-wedeln. You will have the impression that your heels are slipping back and forth much more than the ski tips; and most important, that all the action takes place below your bent knees. (Naturally, you'll mark the rhythm of these blurred micro turns with your poles, just as in any series of short turns.) It's critical that you practice, and get the hang of lower-leg swiveling on flat slopes before you try it in the bumps. This is not a powerful, almost universal technique like the dynamic anticipation we've spent so much time on. These are slight,

FIG. 5.5 SUPER-ANTICIPATION OR "LOWER LEG SWIVELING."
*One of the bump skier's secret weapons. Extremely rapid
pivoting of the lower leg—below the knees! Invaluable in tight,
kinky bumps, this super-anticipation can also be easily
practiced (as shown here) on flat slopes, or on catwalks.*

quick, almost decorative turns that rely on helpful terrain (either smooth and flat, or synchronized with the lip of a bump as a natural pivot point). But because so little of the body is actually moving, such turns are indeed outrageously fast—and if you're primarily using the shape of the bump to turn with and around, you really don't need any more force.

As you try this lower-leg pivoting for quick changes of direction in the midst of tight small bumps, you should no longer bother to shift weight from turn to turn. Reason: there just isn't enough time. When you change rhythm from quick pivots back to longer full turns, the arc of the turn itself will help put your weight back where it belongs, on the outside ski. And to some extent, as you become increasingly subtle at reading and using the moguls to your advantage, more and more of your active turning will be of this lower-leg variety. There are lots of situations where the bump skier feels tall and loose, almost floating over the snow, where only the feet appear to be working. In other words, as you use the terrain more knowledgeably, the focus of action tends to lower, ever closer to the skis. Check this out by watching the handful of gifted, dedicated, fanatical bump skiers that you'll always find on the area's hardest, steepest mogul runs. When viewed from below, their whole bodies seem motionless, right down to the knees; only their lower legs move laterally from one turn to the next. Of course, such skiers are usually locked in the fall line, skiing the short, fast line, barely turning when you think about it—and lower leg action is all they need. In any case, it's a great skill to add to your quiver. (Note that I've only said that the upper legs or thighs *appear* motionless. In this technique—which the great French coach, Georges Joubert, tried to baptize "surf technique" with a truly Gallic sense of the absurd—the femur actually rotates in the hip socket around its long axis. But that's a matter for ski technicians to split hairs over.)

So much for quickness. Now what are we going to do about badly shaped bumps? Depends. The first case to consider is that of bumps with an exceptionally sharp, cut-off sort of lip that drops you into a steep, fairly narrow and not at all rounded gully. Here it's a problem of balance and speed control. The sharper the lip, the more you have to *drop the tips of your skis* in order to hug the slope on the other side. This "tip drop" in bumps is a funny move because, although it feels as though you are pressing your toes down to keep the ski tips on the snow, you also wind up lifting the tails with a sort of knee-bending that actually tucks your feet up underneath you. Never mind, it works so long as you concentrate on pressing toes and tips down over the lip of the bump. And this puts you in a good position to use the most obscure and hard to explain speed-control mechanism of all, a kind of vertical sideslip down the steep and narrow trough.

By vertical sideslip, I mean that your skis are not turned across the hill, but *angled steeply down it.* Weight stays on your heels (because if you weighted the fronts of your skis, they would start to curve around and hit the side of the gully). And in this steeply angled position you scrape down the gully on your edges, slowing down a bit in the process without ever letting yourself turn until things finally widen out below the actual bump. A bit confusing? Well, I told you it was hard to explain! But perhaps with these clues you can discover for yourself how to sideslip with your skis pointed almost straight down, and not turning. (If you've ever flown a light plane, the feeling is similar to crabbing sideways with right rudder and left aileron—unnatural but effective.) When normally rounded gullies become steep narrow chutes, this may be all the braking effect you can get for a while. So it's a good ace to have up your sleeve.

The next nasty shape to consider is the mogul whose flanks and gullies are completely blocked by one of those mini-cliffs or chopped-off walls. There's usually a bit of room to squeeze by over on the far side, against the flank of the next bump. But this line, very long, stretched out and rounded, requires that you consciously delay the pivoting action of your skis down the hill. Start such turns as usual from an anticipated position on the crest of your bump, but instead of letting your skis pivot, extend the top (outside) foot forward, across the hill, as if reaching out for the next bump to the side. This delays the start and gets your skis far enough out to the side so that they can pivot around the mini-cliff—instead of over it, *thump!* This extra-long round line is a bit unnerving at first, but it smooths out drop-offs in the terrain too abrupt to be absorbed—and in the long run it will save your back and knees. Which brings us to our last horror mogul.

This is the real no-exit bump whose gully closes out in a V-shaped slot—desperate and terrifying because you know it's going to trap you and squirt your skis out over the next lip and into the next abyss (which, if you're un-lucky, will end in yet another V-slot!). Faced with such a monster, you have only two choices. Bail out, turn aside onto the front face or nose of the bump, which is normally just where you don't want be, and make a few quick pivots, moving sideways to find a better line. Or, a braver solution: try for maximum absorption by stretching out as tall as possible before you hit the bottom of the V-slot, then allow your knees to be pushed up almost to your chest, and reextend as fast as possible as you squirt out over the next lip. Turning in the normal sense stops here, although the slots may be angled slightly from one side to the other. It's more of a hit and bounce phenome-non, with as much absorption as you can man-age to soften the blows. Why bother? A good question. In my view, only because after two or three of these monsters, there's always a rounder line you can ski out to one side or the other, in order to slow down and ease your way back into more graceful skiing.

Grace, fluidity, lightness . . . these are the real attributes of good bump skiing. Unfortunately, they have nothing to do with the skiing style that creates the drop-off type of ugly bump described earlier. Those mini-walls barring the bottom of many bumps are produced by the nervous overpivoting of intermediates who have strayed into the bumps over their heads, only to pay the price in a panicky, uncomfortable descent. A small sin, easily forgiven—and whose results can easily be avoided by skiing a better, more efficient and graceful line. Not so, the awful V-slot bumps; these are produced by very strong, gifted skiers who try to show off by skiing as brutal and violent a line as possible. They pay a different price. After a half-dozen years of such violent skiing (hit and bounce, hit and bounce) these warriors generally retire from the lists with permanent back damage and/or destroyed knee joints, and years of pain ahead of them. Don't be suckered into skiing like this because it "looks cool." But don't be frightened to cope with the desperate moguls such skiers leave, either. These worst of all moguls are seldom continuous. If you find yourself trapped in such a line, you can almost always get out of it in a couple of turns.

The rest should be poetry in motion. Bump skiing is not only the greatest challenge you can find at most ski areas. It's also one of the most outrageous, exciting and just plain beautiful forms of skiing, period. When every-

FIG. 5.6 RADICAL MOVES IN BUMPS. *In high-level bump skiing no two turns are exactly alike. Legs fold and unfold. The body is always in a state of extreme but relaxed anticipation. Skis follow the terrain, using the gullies more often than the faces of the bumps.*

thing comes together in the bumps, as in all high-level skiing, time slows down, your senses expand, the world you're dancing through becomes infinitely richer. For bump skiing at its best is a dance: a demanding, gymnastic sort of dance, a jazz dance compared to the dreamy waltz of powder, but still a dance. The technique, the tricks we've gone over here, are only the steps, the dotted lines on the tilted moguled floor of our cosmic mountain ballroom. You supply the feelings. Will your bump skiing adventures be smooth or brutal, light or heavy, supple or powerful, relaxed or stiff? Your choice. A choice you can constantly refine, but always a new adventure.

- *The most common problem in bump skiing is an overpivoted, too rapid start to the turn, which leads to the skis getting stuck crosswise in the gully, or cutting back too soon into the bump with no room to finish the turn.*

- *The classic, effective bump turn involves a slow anticipated start on the crest of the bump, a rounded progressive entry into the gully, a positive finish to the turn on the (generally) flat area below the bump.*

- *Maintain your anticipation, timing and rhythm from turn to turn by reaching straight down the hill for the next bump with the tip of your outside pole.*

● *The average bump offers the skier a choice of two exits from the turn: a fast exit just below the bump, or a slow one, turning up and over the next bump to the side. Use these two possibilities to vary your line and control your speed.*

● *Terrain absorption is important only at higher speeds or in very mean bumps. Hitting the crest of a bump will fold your legs for you; the skier must concentrate on reextending for the next bump.*

● *For super-quick bump turns, use "super-anticipation" or the rapid pivoting of the lower legs and skis* beneath the knees.

6

CARVING, SLICING AND HOLDING

Skiing with Precision from Hardpack to Ice

The memory is as clear as yesterday: a World Cup Giant Slalom on the face at Heavenly Valley. A cold clear morning, Lake Tahoe below us reflecting a cloudless blue sky, the race course steep and icy. Above all, icy. The Heavenly Valley crew had been working for weeks to create this ice: watering the slope, scraping, smoothing, raking it, and then watering it again, night after night. We had come to watch, to photograph, gawk at and learn from the best of the best. But standing on skis beside the course was a challenge in itself. The slope was so unbelievably icy that even standing still you felt as if your skis would slip out from under you at any moment. A spectator's glove, dropped on the slope, slid 500 feet out of sight. The iciest ice I'd ever seen! The forerunners, a handful of the best young Class A racers in California, came down this course like certified spastics: eyes wide as saucers, skidding twenty feet sideways on each turn, hanging on for dear life. And then the first seed racers—the heroes of the day, Ingemar Stenmark, Bojan Krijaz, Heini Hemmi. . . . They were like skiers from another world. It was as though they were skiing on packed powder, no chattering, no skidding, carving perfect round lines on a bulletproof, mirrorlike surface—ultimate carved turns! I had just seen a vision of the possible on skis that far exceeded my imagination. Precision skiing at a level that ordinary skiers might never approach, but still the sort of inspiration that lasts for years. That's still with me today.

Is happiness really a carved turn? A turn with no skidding whatever, where the outside ski leaves a crisp, razor-thin track in the snow? As usual the answer is a resounding *yes, no,* and *maybe.* A few years back, carved turns were all the rage. Instructors only wanted to teach carved turns, only wanted to ski carved turns. Coaches only coached carved turns. Ski writers only wrote about carved turns. Much of the rationale for this enthusiasm stemmed from the belief that carved turns were the fastest way to change direction, and hence the absolute be-all and end-all of racing technique. Today coaches and racers alike have realized that in many situations a carved turn is not the fastest way to change directions in a race course. So carved turns have lost a little of their luster. But only a little, because they are still wonderfully efficient, the hallmark of a highly polished technique, and still beautiful to look at. And above all, because carved turns feel so incredibly satisfying—a delicious, precise sensation underfoot.

Skiers readily speak of "floating" in powder snow, but for me carving is a form of floating on the pack. When carving, I feel light, deft, energized—sublimely pleased. When I ski for myself rather than for a class of less experienced skiers, I focus much of my awareness on what my skis are doing on the snow, feeling whether they are carving or skidding. All my skier's senses seem concentrated along the edge of my ski, and I love nothing better than to leave my signature on the slope in a series of perfectly carved arcs.

Carving gives you an extra dimension of control over your skis—the same sort that figure skaters exhibit in their beautifully precise school figures. Yet carved turns aren't formal figures, they can be free and spontaneous, applied, stretched, compressed at will, on almost any slope, at almost any speed. The ability to carve lets you ski with confidence when our snowy playgrounds metamorphose into sheets of ice, as they sometimes do. And carving is, finally, an ultimate confirmation of what expert skiing is all about: a sign of excellence, a proof of skill and subtlety inscribed in the snow by the edge of your ski. Comparing a series of perfectly carved arcs to a sloppy semi-skidded run is like comparing dancing to jogging.

But before we take a closer look at the sometimes elusive world of carved turns, let me repeat a point I made back in chapter two.

It's never a black and white world, never either/or. Turns are not either purely carved or purely skidded, but more or less carved or more or less skidded. A continuous spectrum exists between the perfect, pure carved turn— a sort of fiction that one can approach but never quite reach—and the totally skidded change of direction in which the ski behaves like an awkward two-by-four.

If you've followed the logic of *Breakthrough on Skis* thus far, and have mastered the key skills that produce this breakthrough into expert skiing, then you're already making somewhat carved turns. In chapter two, "The Arc of the Turn," we learned about the two factors that make a weighted ski want to turn on its own. The ski's side-cut, with the tip much wider than waist and tail, makes the ski "grip" up front and lets the tail slide sideways: this is the effect that produces skidded turns. On the other hand, the ski's narrow waist permits it to bend into reverse camber: the arched shape that is responsible for carving. So far so good, this stuff is old hat for you.

Skiing exclusively on the outside foot, one of the basics of expert technique, has helped you to squeeze the maximum reverse camber out of your skis. And early weight shift, or pre-weighting the uphill ski before turning, has made it difficult if not impossible to overtwist or overpivot the turning ski. All this has contributed to a style of turning that is already more carved than skidded. Your arcs are round. The tracks you leave in the snow are reasonably narrow, not wide, sideways blurs. Instead of starting from scratch as most inter-mediate/advanced skiers must do when they want to learn how to carve, you're almost there. All you need now is a bit more subtlety and refinement, a few small tricks, and you'll be able to carve a very pure arc indeed. But where, exactly, will you use this precision skill?

First and foremost, carving is a cruising skill: suitable, appropriate and unbelievable fun to do in wide, large turns at pretty fair speeds. Trying to carve makes much less sense in rapid short turns on steeper slopes (which, as we'll discover, is extremely dif-ficult). And as we've just seen in the last chap-ter, carving makes no sense at all in the bumps. The icier the slope, the harder it is to really carve—but as conditions approach true boilerplate, the skills of carving will still keep you on your feet, and on your line, while most other skiers are skidding haplessly toward the trees. But enough generalizations, let's get specific.

A Carving Primer: Subtlety, Edging and the Tail of the Turn

My advice on carving consists equally of do's and don't's. The biggest no-no, of course, is an overpivoted initiation. The ideal start to a carved turn (not always possible) involves no pivoting whatsoever, simply a weight shift to the top foot, and a slow, gentle rolling of that top/outside ski over onto its new edge. There

FIG. 6.1 THE MIDDLE OF A CLASSIC CARVED TURN. An exercise in precise balance. The skier stands on the edge of his outside foot, neither forward nor back, but as much as possible centered over the carving ski, feeling the ski bend and grip throughout its entire length.

is virtually no anticipation and the turn itself is caused by the ski slowly bending and peeling off into a pure carved arc. Indeed, there's a moment of delicious hesitation, of real uncertainty, at the start of a pure carved turn, where you simply have to wait . . . wait . . . for a long split second before the ski begins to turn. The first rule, then, is *minimum motion*—no strong twisting. The second is to use extreme subtlety in whatever movements you do make. And this *quietness* is especially important at the start of a turn.

Why is the start critical? At first, this doesn't make sense because if your skis are going to wash out, break sideways off their edges and skid, they will inevitably do so at the tail end of the turn. That's because the main forces acting on the skier, centrifugal force and gravity, tend to gang up and amplify each other in the last third of any turn, pulling you sideways much harder than they did in the first third, or middle of the arc. As a result, any small tendency to skid at the top of the turn will be magnified manyfold at the end. Hence my emphasis on a quiet, subdued, almost motionless initiation if you really want to carve a pure arc. Any rambunctious behavior, any excess pivoting at the start will be paid for in spades, turning into a big skid at the bottom of your arc.

But although the start is critical, the tail of the turn is the payoff, the real moment of truth. This is where the real action, the real skill, the true pleasure of a carved turn is found. When

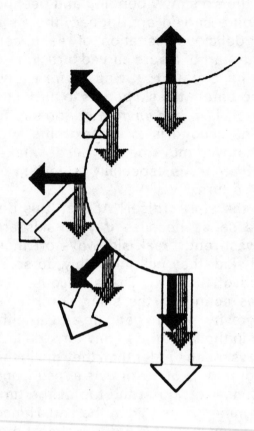

FIG. 6.2 WHY SKIS TEND TO SKID OUT AT THE END OF TURNS. *Two main forces act on the skier and the skis: gravity (which is always pulling down the slope, shown here as a striped arrow); and centrifugal force (pulling outward from the arc of the turn, shown here as a black arrow). In the first half of the turn these two forces tend to cancel each other out; in the second half they gang up on the skier—lining up in the same direction and producing a much greater resultant force (shown as a white arrow) that tends to push the skis sideways into a skid.*

FIG. 6.3 THE TAIL END OF A CARVED TURN. Here the skier deals with the problem of increased sideways force at the end of the turn by progressively increasing the pressure on the tail of the ski. Often the carved turn is completed by carving on the tail of the ski alone. The most efficient way to accomplish this rearward transfer of pressure is probably through a forward push of the outside foot (between the second and third figures).

I look to see how truly proficient a skier is, I always concentrate my attention on the end rather than the start of his or her turns. And so, of course, the subtlety of movement—or is it *non*movement?—that I recommended for the initiation must be carried through the whole turn. Consider, for example, the arm/hand/pole position in a pure carved turn:

Every accomplished skier has developed a sort of "home-base" position for the hands—usually somewhat spread and ahead of the hips. With your hands in this position, your weight seems naturally distributed across the whole length of the turning foot, evenly spread from toe to heel. But if you move your outside hand ahead, even six inches from this home-base position near the end of a carved turn on hard snow—wham! the tails of your skis break loose and skid. Moving your outside hand has, in effect, redistributed more weight to the front of your boot, overloaded the tip and lightened the tail of your turning ski. And presto, you've lost your carve. Likewise, if you drop your outside hand back behind your hips. This small movement overloads the heel of your boot and the tail of your ski, which again breaks away in a sudden skid. It's amazing what a difference a small hand movement can make in the ski's ability to carve a clean arc. The outside hand of your turn, in particular, seems critical here. Don't wave it around if you want to carve!

The lesson is clear: to carve a pure arc, the curved edge of the ski needs to bite and hold equally along its whole length. And this brings us to the idea of edging in a carved turn. How much edging do you need to carve a pure arc? A tongue-in-cheek answer might be: more edge than you think. A more accurate response: it all depends. It depends on how long or short a turn you're trying to carve. The carving action of a ski comes from reverse camber —the bending of the ski into an arc. Just how much the ski bends when you stand on it depends directly on its edge angle. As the ski tilts up more on its edge, the narrow waist can be pushed into a deeper arc before contacting the snow. So more edge equals more reverse camber, which equals a shorter turn. This means that to shorten a carved turn, all you need to do is increase the edge angle of your ski.

Whatever the size of your carved turn, you will still be riding an edged ski—whether slightly or strongly edged—and to do this you want to stand *on the inside edge of your foot.* This is one factor that really distinguishes carving from lazy semi-skidded turns. In bump skiing, for example, we saw how a relaxed foot helps the ski to slip and slide through the troughs. Carving is the exact opposite. You tighten the muscles in your foot until you can feel a line of pressure (your weight) distributed along the *inside edge* of your sole. Don't over do it and give yourself cramps. You want just enough tension in the turning foot to let you stand solidly on the edge of your ski—less tension on softer packed-powder, progressively more as the snow hardens toward ice. This standing on the edge of the foot will be a new feeling for some, quite natural for others; but easy to achieve once you think of it.

All the same, there's more to subtle, efficient edging than just standing on the edge of your foot. In skiing's strange vocabulary, the action that edges the skis is often called *angulation*—some adjustment of the body from its normal straight up-and-down position. Rapid increases in edge angle can best be obtained by pushing the knees forward and in (knee angulation). A nice way, for instance, to shorten the radius of a carved turn. A less rapid but stronger method of achieving the edge angle you need in a given turn is to get your skis out to the side, away from your body (often called hip angulation because the hips seem to be so dramatically inboard of the skis). In practice you can let your hips drop to the inside of the turn, *or* you can let your feet and legs slip out to the outside during the start of the turn. Or best of all, simply let your skis move into this edged (angled out to the side) position via whatever combination of body adjustments comes naturally, without thinking too much about how you do it. Just focus on the amount of edging you need for a given turn. This is one case where you have to trust the old bod to do its thing.

What else can aid the skis' tendency to carve? The only other hot tips I have to offer are a couple of tricks for improving that always tenuous tail end of a carved turn. We've learned that the skier's weight should be distributed equally along the entire length of the ski, from tip to midsection to tail, so that each part carves and holds equally. Ideally, but not in practice. Since the tails of the skis are not as wide as the tips, they never grip the snow quite as strongly as the fronts of the skis—which is why, at some point near the end of the turn, they tend to break away in more of a skid. The solution is simple: apply increased pressure to the tail of the ski during the very last part of your turn to make it grip a little more ("rear leverage" in our ski-technical jargon).

How to do this? Several options: Just settling back on your heels may sometimes work, especially in easygoing, long-radius carved turns at medium speeds; but it's not a very satisfying option. Any sitting back position is muscularly fatiguing, stresses and tires your quads, and limits your range of motion and flexibility. The trick is to *transfer pressure* to the tail of the ski without moving your weight backward. An ingenious way to do this—which I learned years ago from former U.S. Ski Team coach Dick Dorworth—is to simply tighten the hamstrings (the muscles at the rear of your thigh) in your active leg. In essence, this levers your foot back in the boot and transfers strong tail pressure that keeps the ski from washing out in the last part of its carved arc. An equally effective move—and a more versatile one as we'll soon see—is to *push your outside foot forward* in the last third of the turn. Given the design of modern ski boots, it's almost impossible to push your foot very far forward beneath you. But the action of pushing, or of trying to push, the outside boot forward through the end of the turn is an effective way of transferring pressure to the heel. And it leads to a whole new technique for making the skis hold, *slicing,* which we'll look at next.

Above all, don't try to use all these suggestions at once! Just experiment with one or the other, from time to time, to see what feels good, what works for you. However you do it —and there is no one right way—you'll begin to finish your carved turns with more pressure on the inside of your heel. Let this pressure build up as you feel the pressures of the turn build. And *voilà,* your skis will hold as never before, carving cleanly around as far as you want.

I ought to add that my advice to experiment with these different moves—one at a time, not all at once—applies to all the different aspects of carving turns that we've just discussed. Spend a morning focusing on quieting down your long-radius turn initiation until it's almost motionless. Another day, concentrate on the sensations of edging in the soles of your feet, and play with different edge angles, observing the various results. Finally, on yet another occasion, work on the feeling of transferring pressure to the tails at the end of your carved turns. Carving is not one technique but a combination of subtle factors that enhance your skis' response. Try to do it all, all at once, and you'll only achieve a muddle: mental and physical overload that translates into lousy turns. Carving really involves building a deeper rapport with the edges of your skis. And such intimate friendship takes time to nurture.

Slicing: The Role of Forward Foot Thrust

Slicing is a natural outgrowth of carving—one step beyond—that comes into play when the carved turn reaches its limits. Classical carving is a thing of balance and beauty in medium-to-long-radius turns; but in short turns, good luck! By their nature short turns require a lot of initial twisting or pivoting of the skis. Well, naturally, this initial twisting (or untwisting) is going to amplify into a fair amount of skidding by the end of the turn. And once you're skidding sideways, there's no use edging harder. It's too late. What to do?

Slicing is the answer, a very particular technique that will give you a certain amount of carving, even at the tail end of a short turn, even on ice. By slicing I mean *the forward push or forward thrust of the outside ski.* This is a very modern move in expert skiing—something that works wonders but which, like skiing one hundred percent on the outside ski, is not easy to observe. Let me try explain it by an analogy: Trying to slice a tomato with a dull knife is a tough job. Push straight down on the tomato skin and nothing happens. But if you slice the knife forward across the tomato skin, it begins to cut. The same thing happens with skis.

In an earlier period of skiing, *edgesets* were all the vogue: slamming one's knees, ankles and edges straight in toward the slope, in order to stop the skidding at the end of one turn and provide a platform from which to rebound into the next. This style of edging—with the edges biting straight down into the snow like that dull knife into the tomato—is seldom used today except on very steep slopes (see chapter eight, "Extreme Dimensions of Expert Skiing"). Instead, the best skiers create forward sliding or slicing platforms at the end of their turns with a forward push of their skis.

As I mentioned, this movement is all but invisible, since the forward tilt of the modern boot prevents one from pushing it very far ahead. But even when it's brief and minimal, a forward push of the foot will make the ski's edge slice deeper into the snow—with the most interesting results. We've already seen that a gentle, steady forward push of the foot can build up tail pressure and help you hold your carve through the last few degrees of a big turn. Similarly, at the end of a short turn, a sudden vigorous forward thrust of the feet can bring all skidding to an end, slicing you out of one arc and into the next. And note, please, that I've talked almost interchangeably of pushing your foot and pushing your feet. Typically, both feet will move forward but only the outside, weighted foot really counts.

Foot thrust is not necessarily reserved for

slicing at the end of the turn. We know that in expert skiing the end of one turn typically blends seamlessly into the start of the next, and foot push can help here too. In certain snow conditions at reasonably fast speeds, pushing the outside ski ahead at the very start of the turn can initiate carving on the tail much sooner and eliminate any tendency to over-turn. Even in bumps, I sometimes push my feet forward, both to slow down the initiation and to bring my skis into contact with the far wall of the gully where I want to bank a longer turn. And foot thrust can sometimes be a legitimate help in powder as you'll see in chapter seven.

You might be wondering if this foot thrust won't leave you in an unbalanced, sitting-back position. Fortunately it doesn't. At the end of a turn your skis are slowing down anyway, so your body will catch up. And at the start, your body will typically cross over the skis and take a kind of shortcut trajectory down the hill, still keeping up.

What I'm saying is that slicing, pushing your feet ahead, is an expert's option. A move to be employed from time to time in a wide variety of different circumstances. I can't specify when to use this intriguing option, nor how much, nor how fast. But I can encourage you to play with it, and by trial and error make it your own. You can overdo slicing, and you can use it inappropriately. I'm sure you will. But you'll also feel some great new sensations underfoot as the skis slice forward in situa-tions where normally they would be starting to skid sideways. So try slicing from time to time. You'll love it—although it may take you, as it did me, several seasons of experimentation before you feel comfortable doing it.

Is Ice Nice? Holding on the Super-Slick

Ice is a relative thing. A western skier's "boilerplate" may be a Vermonter's "hardpack." I once skied Snowbird, Utah, with a local instructor who was very apologetic about the "icy" conditions—which I considered lovely packed powder. And so it goes. But all of us have skied ice, slipped and slid, fallen and cursed. If all skiing took place on ice, it would never have become the popular sport it is today. Most skiers, even very good skiers, are content to cope with ice; few dream of mastering it. And yet the damn stuff can be skied. Skied well. All it requires are perfectly tuned skis, a subtle and precise technique, and a strategy that takes into account how hard and slippery an icy ski slope really is.

First things first. You don't have a chance on ice without sharp edges—truly sharp! Serious icy conditions mean sharpening your skis (or having them sharpened) every day. In fact, during particularly icy periods at some of the ski resorts where I've lived and worked, I found the only way I could cope was to go in at lunch and resharpen my skis for the afternoon. That's not quite accurate: it wasn't so much a question of coping with the ice, but of skiing my very best on it. When sharpening skis for ice, it's often a good idea not to deburr the edges after filing them. The microscopic jaggedness of the burr left by the file actually helps cut into the ice. Well-prepared skis are always a delight to ski on, and a reasonably important part of expert skiing. But there are many friendly conditions, of the packed-powder variety, where perfectly prepared skis are not really essential. Ice isn't one of them, though, and without perfectly sharp edges you won't even get to first base.

But here's the surprise. Although you need very sharp edges, the commonest problem in skiing ice is *overedging.* It's a natural reaction, I suppose, when you feel yourself skidding sideways across the slick to try to dig in with those edges and stop the slide. Too late. Instead, you can often recover by relaxing your feet a little and diminishing the edge to the point where it can hold a bit. In almost every situation on ice the basic idea is to use as little edging as you can possibly get away with, the absolute minimum edge angle that will do the job. Experts often speak of "feathering" their edges on ice—and I find it a nice image. Ice is one situation where less is indeed more. I have a few specific suggestions about using those edges, gently yet effectively on ice, but first a couple of generalities.

Everything I said about subtle movements in carving goes double for skiing ice. The essential problem of an icy ski slope is that it offers no resistance to your movements. So any big movements will have unexpected and exaggerated consequences. All movement has to be reduced to a subtle, quiet minimum. The pivoting force needed to initiate a short turn in sticky spring snow, for instance, might be enough to spin you around 360 degrees on an icy surface.

Realizing that sudden moves of any kind have unpleasant consequences on ice, you also want to eliminate sudden turns. This means, on the one hand, looking further ahead to plan your line, and on the other, stretching all your turns out—as round, as slow and as long as you can fit into the space available. Stretch your short turns out into medium-radius arcs, your medium turns into long ones, and you'll be far less likely to start sliding sideways. Likewise, don't complete your turns as far out of the fall line as usual. Even a little experience on ice suffices to give you a kind of sixth-sense warning that your tails are about to break away in a skid. Before that happens, start a new turn by getting off your downhill ski.

When the steepness or narrowness of the trail forces you into shorter turns, your best chance of holding is to use that forward slicing action of the outside foot, just when you feel your skis about to let go. Indeed, that forward push of the feet we've called slicing is a valuable secret weapon in almost all turns on ice—and is sometimes the only way you can make your edges grip—but unfortunately icy slopes are not the best place to learn this move.

So back to edges: To help your edges grip

the ice, try to do everything as delicately as possible. This means not only using the least edge that will do the job, but also avoiding any sudden build-up of pressure on the edge of the ski that will overload its rather minimal grip and send it off in a sideways skid. Ski like a cat, light and delicate on your feet. As if you were skiing on acres of fresh eggs, trying not to break a single one. And avoid turning your skis at much of an angle to your direction of motion. If you can keep the ski slicing more or less forward most of the time, the cutting and holding power of the edge will increase. To keep your skis from overturning on the slick, you'll also want to ski with more heel pressure than normal—not just at the end of the turn but throughout the arc. This neutralizes the grabbiness of the ski's wider tip and helps keep the tails from constantly washing out sideways.

Occasionally a ski slope may become so hard and icy that we have to break the number one rule of expert skiing—standing predominantly on one foot. The skier's weight is too much for the tenuous grip of the edge and breaks the ski loose into a skid. In this case ski *lightly,* very lightly, and *equally on both skis.* It may just work since each edge has to support only half the weight, resist half the force.

Finally, in those snowless transition weeks, when an area's hardpack is slowly being scraped down and compressed into ice, try to be aware of where the remaining soft snow is being deposited. Especially in icy bumps, you'll often find patches of loose scraped-off snow deposited against the top flank of the next bump down the hill. By slowing down your turns in such situations, delaying the initiation and waiting to complete the arc until you have dropped down to that berm of scraped snow, you can wind up skiing on snow while others around you are slipping on solid ice. Cunning use of terrain shapes, be they moguls, hillocks or natural rolls, can also make your life easier on ice. Finishing a turn on a fall-away in the slope will only accentuate the skis' tendency to skid out. On the other hand, finishing a turn against a large bump or roll will help keep the skis from skidding out.

And one last hint. Be easy on yourself. Don't demand too much perfection, too much precision on ice. Carving skills will help you deal with the slick but they won't tame it for you. Think of ice as a terribly demanding final exam for your mastery of the "carving curriculum," where a fifty-percent success rate is a triumph. When helping inexperienced intermediates cope with ice I always suggest that once their skis have begun to slip, they should simply relax, spread their feet for balance, and enjoy the skid. Eventually they'll hit a patch of less icy snow where life will return to normal. Even with real experts, clinicing other instructors on icy slopes, I try to keep things light and reasonable. Setting impossibly high goals for precise skiing on ice just sets one up for failure. Skiing the slick is an ongoing challenge that you can only get better at, never truly master. But at least it isn't boring.

- *The most important factor in carving turns is a slow, progressive initiation to the turn. Avoid overpivoting like the plague.*

- *Feel yourself standing on the inner edge of your outside, weighted foot. As the turn finishes, transfer pressure to the inside of your heel which will help the tail of the ski to "grip" and not wash out. This becomes more important the further you carve out of the fall line.*

- *Slicing is the forward thrusting or pushing of the outside foot. This can make the ski continue to carve well past the point where it would normally break loose and skid out. Slicing is most useful at the very end of a turn, in conditions (very icy or steep) where carving is difficult.*

- *Ice requires incredibly well-tuned, extra-sharp skis, plus extremely quiet and restrained movements. Avoid overedging; use the minimum edge angle that will hold.*

- *Utilize changing shapes in the terrain and patches of scraped-off softer snow to minimize the problem of skidding on icy surfaces. Keep smiling.*

7

FIRST TRACKS

Skiing the Deep from Powder to Sierra Cement

You heard it on the early A.M. ski report: "Eighteen inches of new snow at the top of the mountain, 12 at midway." And outside your window the world is new, fresh, covered in white. Your friends can't wait, there's a crazy excitement in the air. But you're still a bit nervous. It's not like you ski a lot of powder. At most you get two one-week ski vacations out west every year, but some seasons it doesn't snow at all. And the last time you tried powder—well, it seemed like you never made more than three turns before a hidden land mine got you. . . . Later, at the top of the mountain it's worse. Open bowls of fresh trackless white, a real invitation, something out of a ski movie, too perfect to mess up with the hesitant, halfhearted tracks you're afraid you'll leave behind. But other skiers don't hesitate. They pass you and fan out into the virgin snow with whoops and hollers of delight. The powder flies over their heads; their tracks serpentine down out of sight. First tracks. By the time you're ready there may not be any untracked snow left. . . .

Skiing deep powder is more than just another variation on the theme of expert skiing—in many ways it's the *summum,* the max, the ne plus ultra, the emotional high point of any skier's experience. Powder is such a high that it's often compared to sex, to drugs, to flying. Powder skiing feels the way one imagines having wings might feel, the way we all dreamed of flying as children. A dream come true.

The mystique of powder skiing is so widespread and so hyped-up that virtually every skier has run into it. And this mystique, this gushing enthusiasm about skiing the deep is a real source of frustration and irritation to skiers who haven't made their peace with powder. "All right already," one wants to say, "knock it off, nothing can be *that* good!" Wrong. It's that good—and better.

Powder, the real thing, is not just a dusting of new snow. A few inches over a packed surface look great, feel great, but no, they don't really count as deep snow, because one is actually skiing on the hard surface beneath the new stuff. Powder skiing begins with around ten inches to a foot of new snow on the ground, deep enough so that one is no longer standing on the usual solid surface but, instead, floating somewhere *within* the snow. This sensation of floating is a special state that skiers experience only in powder. And deep powder, the very raw material of myth, begins somewhere around eighteen inches of fluff, knee-deep or deeper. An alien universe for most skiers.

Fortunately, skiing deep snow is not at all hard to *do,* although it often seems amazingly hard to *learn.* For me, as for most good skiers, deep snow is an easier, more forgiving, more relaxing medium than hardpack. You just ski it, that's all. There's no question of skiing it better or worse, of perfecting your turns or your line, of that endless, infinite fine-tuning that is possible on hard snow or ice. Yet my years of teaching have demonstrated that there is a real barrier to overcome, an awkward transition, a painful initiation, before one can relax into the powder experience. Learning to ski the deep is somehow much harder than learning to ski on a packed surface; but once learned, it's definitely easier to do—the powder paradox. Here's why, and also a method to short-circuit this frustrating initiation period.

The problem is one of balance, stance and familiarity. Powder offers the skier a nonsurface to stand in, not a solid surface to stand on. Deep snow does indeed compress beneath your skis until it supports your weight, but this base is tenuous, moving, shifting. You rise and sink, you float—and all too often you wobble. Often too, your skis, hidden beneath an opaque white blanket, exhibit alarming tendencies to go off on their own, in different directions. So the whole trick to learning powder is really this: Instead of rushing in and trying to ski it, take the time first to become comfortable in this new medium. Learn to stand, steady and unshakable, before you learn to turn. Balance, stance and stability in deep snow are quite different than on the pack. And the whole key to your success in powder will be to put stability before mobility. Like this:

The powder skier stands solidly on *both* feet, *equally weighting* both skis. I know this contradicts everything I've said so far about experts always skiing on the outside ski—but think of it as the exception that proves the rule. The reason is simple. In deep snow, equally weighted skis will compress the snow beneath them equally, and both will float at the same level. Stand on one ski more than the other (or exclusively) and it sinks, submarining beneath the snow, while the other, lighter ski diverges, floating to the top. A problem for the skier akin to that of trying to straddle two horses going in opposite directions. Inevitably, a flailing desperate recovery or a face plant results.

This is such a change from the stance you've built up—the one-footed balance that has brought you into the world of expert skiing —that you should spend a while, a few runs at least, just cruising straight through easy powder, not steep, not scary, getting used to this new way of standing. If I can persuade you to blast straight through some easy, low-angle powder snow without trying to turn until you begin to feel really comfortable standing equally on both skis, then I will have saved you many hours of frustration. As an instructor, I've invented a thousand excuses and stratagems to distract my powder students from the fact that, no, they weren't yet turning, while together we gained the necessary mileage and built a steady powder stance, a new kind of balance. In this case, I'll have to rely on your believing me. Don't ruin it by trying to turn too soon.

A few extra tips on the powder stance: The easiest way to insure equally weighted skis is through equally bent legs. And should you find yourself suddenly on one ski, starting to lose it, simply sink down, flexing both legs equally and deeply, which restores equal pressure on both skis, then stand back up. How about sitting back? A real canard, a myth that just won't die in skiing circles, is that you have to sit back in order to make your ski tips float up to the surface. Nonsense. Especially with our modern, softer-flexing skis. If you'll just stand evenly, neither forward nor back, with your weight spread across the flat of both feet, your skis won't dive. I promise. The skis will bend sufficiently in the soft snow for the tips to float up on their own. And any sitting-back position is incredibly fatiguing. Powder skiing is not a pleasure with cramped quads. Granted, in some incredibly tough-to-ski conditions (for example, three feet of heavy, wet, spring glop) a skier may occasionally have to lever back on the tails to free the ski tips. But this is a rare exception. The modern powder skier stands centered, in the middle of both feet, in the center of the skis.

For better balance in powder, spread your arms somewhat wider than normal (always in front of your hips) and use them as a tightrope

FIG. 7.1 THE POWDER STANCE. A basic position for exploring deep snow: feet close together, skis evenly weighted, arms spread wider than normal for increased balance, body more or less upright and relaxed—not in a "sitting back" position, a common skiing myth, which can only lead to fatigue and loss of balance.

walker would, for constant, subtle balance adjustments. Actually, it's not very difficult to get a sense of the special two-footed, floating balance needed for powder. My point here is simply that dealing with a new style of balance *and* a new style of turning at the same time is a bit much. Sensory overload that leads to frustration and failure. Besides, it's great fun just to cut straight through the powder!

You'll discover, among other things, that you can comfortably ski a steeper line than you imagined. This soft fluffy stuff actually slows you down; something you'll use to good effect in serious powder skiing. If the snow is very, very light you can head straight down the fall line on gentler slopes. On steeper pitches, cut across at varying angles. Of course, it's trickier but even more important to keep your weight equal in a traverse than a straight schuss. The heavier and deeper the powder you start practicing in, the steeper a slope you'll have to choose and this will necessitate traversing if you don't want to scare yourself silly.

It doesn't take long. A couple of quick runs, and already you're getting the feel of the powder stance. But this could become boring. It's time to learn to *ski* this stuff.

A New Generation of Skis for Powder

I hope you won't be disappointed when I tell you that it is far easier to master deep snow today than it was when I first wrote *Breakthrough on Skis*. The first super fat powder skis, from Atomic, the Austrian ski manufacturer, appeared in the United States in 1991; now it seems everybody makes a wide powder ski. These fat boys are almost twice as wide as conventional skis! Not the sort of skis one would normally take seriously. Except for one thing. These shorter-than-normal, extra-fat skis make challenging (and even not so challenging) deep snow easy. The deepest powder, the toughest heaviest crud, even dreaded breakable crust. No problem. Really.

Fat skis also simplify the learning process. Technically, everything I describe in this chapter works on these new powder skis, exactly as it does on conventional skis. The only difference is that on fat skis it's almost impossible to screw up. Why? Because of their extreme flotation. With so much surface area, these skis never get trapped beneath the snow. It's hard for many skiers to log enough hours, pay enough dues to feel completely at home in powder. Fat skis are the answer.

Rocky Mountain Fluff:
Learning to Ski Light, Deep Snow

The would-be powder skier will probably begin the adventure in one of two possible worlds: the feather-light, cold, dry and almost weightless snow of the high Rockies (typical of Utah, Idaho, Colorado, Wyoming and Montana), or the heavy, dense, deep snow of the Pacific West (found in the mountains of California, Oregon and Washington). Sure, there's a continuous spectrum of deep snow ranging from ultra light to ultra heavy, but this generalization holds true most of the time. And powder at New England ski areas is so infrequent that you really shouldn't count on it—deep snow skiing is intrinsically a western experience. These two contrasting conditions, light versus heavy powder, are amenable to two different learning approaches. In many ways, lighter Rocky Mountain powder is a friendlier environment and progress thus a bit quicker.

You're already a strong advanced skier, you can link anticipated parallel turns right down the fall line. And you've developed a certain confidence just blasting straight through deep snow without turning. Great. The next step is to find a not too steep slope of untracked or only partly tracked new snow (cut-up powder is always harder to deal with than fresh, untracked stuff). A slope friendly enough that you could actually ski straight down it without turning, or worrying about turning, if push came to shove. Now, starting straight down the fall line, begin first to plant your poles rhythmically—as if you were linking imaginary turns—then, slowly, start to turn your feet and skis a tiny bit from side to side in time with your rhythmic pole plants. As long as you're not trying too hard to turn too much out of the fall line, it will work. This is the spontaneous approach of sneaking yourself into powder skiing without really tackling any specific new skills and it depends one hundred percent on a friendly hill and very light snow.

Note that I said *turn* your feet and skis.

These are active pivoting movements with your muscles doing the work, not effortless arcs due to ski design. After one or two such runs, ease over onto a packed slope and practice the same movements: a continuous fall-line pattern of continuous twists with both feet, both bent legs, standing equally on both skis. Of course it will feel easier and more normal here on a packed slope. Now move back into the fluff and try it again.

You can see where we're headed. Through the backdoor into powder skiing. As the pattern starts to work for you, push it further with progressively steeper slopes, progressively more turning action that will bring your skis farther across the slope. So far so good. But there comes a moment when this spontaneous fall-line approach runs out of steam. Either you encounter snow that's too deep or too dense, too drifted or too windblown, to turn in easily; or else you find yourself on slopes that are too steep, where your moderate fall-line deviations no longer suffice to control your speed. It's time for a few quite specific technical tricks.

As powder slopes steepen and deepen, you'll need both a stronger start and a more powerful finish to each turn. And you'll no longer find it quite as easy to plunge straight down the slope before turning. No use telling yourself that you *ought* to head straight down. Interior alarms will be going off, saying: no, no, no! And you'll find yourself turning from a traverse, although I hope from a fairly steep traverse. When this happens, try the following:

For a more powerful start to your turn, make sure your upper body is strongly anticipated, facing straight downhill, and exaggerate your vertical movement. Begin things with a *rising* movement punctuated by a smart, snappy *lift of your outside hand and pole.* This rising up is nothing more than the formerly familiar "unweighting," once a part of every good turn, but no longer much used or needed on the pack; in deep snow it comes back into its own as a means of liberating the skis from all this extra resistance. The lift of the outside hand, which adds power to the up-unweighting movement, is purely a powder skier's move. It accomplishes wonders in deep snow, but would be a disaster on a packed slope, so beware. On the pack this move would bank the skier far too far to the inside, but in deep snow this very banking helps you turn.

Why? Think of what makes your skis turn in deep snow. Aside from pure muscular twisting, that is. There's no interaction between the edge of the ski and a hard snow surface, so side-cut plays no role. But if the skis themselves are banked, tilted up at an angle against the snow, then the resistance of the powder under their angled bases will push them to the side—much as water skis turn when tilted up against the onrushing water. Okay, that's why banking the body, in order to bank the skis, is a plus in powder—and why lifting the outside hand and pole at the start of the turn works so well! You will be flabbergasted as you lift that hand and feel your skis peel off into a new turn.

There's one more trick that can add power and punch to the start of your turn: *pushing your toes forward, toward the fall line.* This "tip-thrusting" action is a real winner. It's actually pretty subtle, almost invisible, because the shape of modern ski boots prevents us from pushing the feet very far ahead. But the effort of thrusting both feet downhill into the turn more or less guarantees equal weighting and equal flotation at the start of the turn. It also momentarily lightens the ski tips (yet another form of selective unweighting), facilitating their initial pivoting. Luckily, this foot pushing doesn't leave the skier behind, in the dreaded sitting-back position. The resistance of the deep snow always slows the skis sufficiently that the skier's body catches back up in a balanced, centered position.

These two purely powder moves, the snappy lifting of the outside hand and the forward push of both feet, should give you enough power and confidence to launch a strong parallel turn even in the deepest drifts. You'll want to try just one of these moves alone for a while—say, lifting your outside hand. Get used to it before you attempt the other. Don't experiment initially with both at once, although once absorbed these two moves are complementary. None of us can really deal with having two or more physical tasks, goals or movements to work on at the same time.

The stronger powder turn that results will inevitably be a medium-to-long-radius turn. Everything takes longer, you'll discover, in really deep snow, including the time needed to complete a turn. (You'll often feel like an actor in a slow-motion film about powder sking.) Remember to keep your speed up. And remember too that these arcs through the deep stuff are the result both of snow resistance against the banked bottoms of your skis and of continuous leg steering/twisting action. The muscular component need not be a grunt, need not be violent, but it's always there. In powder you guide your skis as much as you ride them. The skier who's used to riding the side-cut around a smooth arc on the pack often gives up and stops turning his legs halfway through a powder turn. When this happens, the skis too stop turning. So a continuous guiding/twisting of the skis through the second half of each turn is part of the stronger finish you need in deeper, steeper snow. For an even stronger finish, if the slope is so steep that you find yourself moving too fast for comfort, finish your turns by pushing the tails of the skis out, away from you, through the snow. (We'll come back to this heel-pushing, leg-extending finish in more detail later.) But you can also err in the direction of overfinishing each turn, and then stall out from loss of speed. Only experience can tell you just how much speed you can

FIG. 7.2 TWO TRICKS FOR THE DEEP. *Two very useful moves that facilitate the start of any turn in deep snow are pushing both feet forward toward the fall line, and a quick vigorous lifting motion of the outside hand. The two work well together, but should first be practiced one at a time.*

carry coming out of each turn. As addicting as the newly found ability to cope with powder is, you'll soon be logging miles and miles of your own tracks in fresh snow.

For this is only the beginning. There is, indeed, a spiffier style of very advanced, highly elegant and relaxed fall-line powder skiing that we'll get to later in this chapter. But your first goal, your first step, is nothing more than stability and coping. Confidence and survival rather than panic in deep snow. Doing it and standing up to tell the tale, doing it however sloppily, rather than daydreaming about doing it. A powder snow initiation in the Rocky Mountains can be both swift and pleasurable because deep snow there is so light, hence so forgiving, that you can make almost every mistake in the book and still get away with it. Not so in the heavier snow of the far west as we're about to discover.

Way Out West: Skiing Heavy, Deep Snow and Sierra Cement

Even though the maritime climate of the Pacific Northwest can produce unbelievably wet, dense, heavy new snow, no nickname has ever stuck to the snows of Mt. Hood, Mt. Rainier, and White Pass, Washington, the way "Sierra cement" has come to describe the California version of heavy powder. It's not a totally accurate label, and yes, pure light fluff does occasionally fall way out west—just as Vail, Aspen and Jackson Hole too can receive occasional blankets of wet, dense glop. But—

and it's an important but—skiing deep snow in the far west is simply a different world. Learning to ski the deep out there is more technical, more challenging, and all things considered, quite a job. Not to worry. You'll become a far better deep-snow skier for it. Because the essence of *heavy* deep snow is that it won't let you get away with any mistakes. Weight one ski exclusively and you've lost it: it's that simple.

A few other remarks just to set the stage. After an overnight dump of three feet in the Lake Tahoe region, for example, only the very steepest slopes are skiable. This is because the resistance of so much dense new snow simply stops you cold on average runs. Skiers may find themselves walking straight down intermediate slopes; and skiing as we know it doesn't really start up again until the snowcats have done their thing. This in turn means that you're forced to start practicing and learning powder technique on slopes steep enough to make even very good skiers nervous. A different ball game with different psychological and technical imperatives. No sneaking in the backdoor here. No one is going to launch themselves straight down the fall line on such steep slopes, gently trying small spontaneous powder turns to either side. It would be instant mind lock, followed by instant head plant.

So the learning strategy changes. The powder apprenticeship in heavy western snow involves starting at the tail end of the turn, mastering a strong finish that really slows you down on such steep slopes; then patiently backing up to the start of the turn before putting together complete powder runs. Like this:

The initial tuning-in period (straight running to develop an unshakable, two-footed powder stance) takes the form of steep traverses, down and across these steep powder-covered slopes. (During the years I taught at Squaw Valley, for example, I found the best powder-teaching terrain to be on the infamously steep slopes of KT-22. Scary, but at least we could move.) You'll end such steep traverses with a very particular form of uphill christy. Sink fairly low on your skis and then, with a twisting extension movement of both legs, push your skis away from you down the hill, thrusting the tails down as you turn the ski tips uphill to stop. To further complicate your life, I want you to do this uphill turn very slowly and progressively. A sudden move in even a foot of heavy snow will snag your skis and you'll topple right over them. Tricky? You bet. Take a second now and reread this paragraph, trying to form a picture of the twisting extension of your legs from a low, bent position— pushing your skis, especially the tails of your skis, *sideways,* away from you, while turning them up the hill. A brand-new move in your skiing repertoire. The skier's secret weapon for the serious steep and deep.

It's not hard, just new. And indeed, it works. Just turning the skis underfoot, with a rotary effort of bent legs, might not accomplish much against the increased resistance of heavy, deep snow. A sideways thrusting extension of the legs is far more powerful and can drive the skis right out through the snow. And now the fun begins, the thrills and chills. Because I'd like to ask you to progressively steepen the angle of each traverse, aiming more and more down the hill, closer and closer to the fall line. Keep your uphill pullout at the end of each traverse slow and smooth, your hands extra-wide for balance; and soon you will be plunging straight down the fall line, gathering speed and then slowly dissipating it in a rounded, uphill arc. Once you can do that—it may take twenty minutes, it may take a whole morning, practicing these steep traverses to both sides—you're home free.

The reason I wanted you to become comfortable, dropping straight down the fall line and then slowly pulling out to a stop, is quite simple. This is exactly the position in which you'll find yourself in the middle of a turn in this steep, heavy powder. And unlike turns on the pack, the skis just don't keep "coming around" on their own—you have to make them come around! That's just what you've been practicing with your uphill christy via twisting extension. As soon as you can pull comfortably out of the fall line to a stop, you're ready to pull off complete downhill turns. And to start these full turns, you'll want to use the two tricks I mentioned in the previous section on Rocky Mountain fluff.

From a fairly steep traverse in a very anticipated position, sink to get ready. Trigger your
turn with the usual pole plant—rise up, lifting
your outside hand smartly, and push both feet
forward into the turn. What a mouthful! What
a turn! The turn I'm proposing for your first
excursions down steep powder faces is not
yet the ideal pattern of expert powder skiing.
Patience. At least I've given you something
that works. Lifting the outside hand and thrusting the feet gets you into the fall line; a twisting extension of the legs brings you out of the
fall line. All these movements are smooth,
slow and powerful, not quick and jerky. (And
this is typical of the slow-motion quality of
deep-snow skiing.) As an extra guarantee of
success, why not practice this turn on the pack
between your forays into the steep and deep.
Once more: a strong lifting (punctuated with
the outside hand) and a forward push of both
feet to begin; then a continued sideways extension of the legs to finish the turn.

I think of this turn as a modern "light
christy" because of its strong unweighting. (A
far cry, to be sure, from the old hallmark turn
of the French National Ski School called the
Christiana Léger.) A turn in which you lift and
float toward the fall line, then sink and press
sideways out of it. A utility turn that lets you
actually ski the deep stuff, and through mileage develop the confidence you'll need for the
higher level approach to powder I'm about to
share with you.

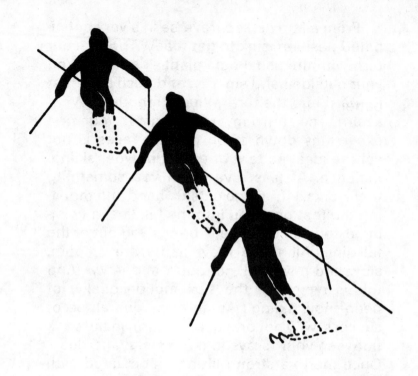

FIG. 7.3 A STRONG FINISH FOR HEAVY POWDER. *Sometimes referred to as "twisting extension," the finish of a turn in heavy powder involves a sideways extension of both legs through the snow, pressing the heels (and ski tails) out away from the skier.*

What's the difference? Experts, of course, don't ski powder one turn at a time. Their turns are typically short, linked arcs; seldom medium-to-long-radius ones. And the rhythm and pattern of their leg action, as we're about to see, is rather different than what I've just described. Then why the detour? Why learn this light christy, this steady, dependable workhorse of a medium-radius turn if we're going to abandon it as we get better? I blush to tell you, it's all part of the powder paradox. The powder turns that are easiest to do are, in fact, hardest to learn. The psychological barriers ("My god, where are my ski tips under all this snow?") and the balance problems (developing a whole new stance) are so great that nine out of ten strong parallel skiers are just unable to drop into the fall line and start linking short turns down through the steep and deep. It comes—but only after one has begun to believe that, yes, I really do belong here, no, I'm not about to crash, yes, I really *can* ski powder.

So now you know. Now you too have become a powder skier. You look back up to the top of the slope and there they are—your own tracks, respectable tracks, not the zigzags and craters of a body-packing descent. Smile, it's a major victory. But those other tracks, those smooth sinuous S's, thin and graceful, show you how far you still have to go before powder skiing is completely your thing. Let's finish the job.

FIG. 7.4 A MODERN "LIGHT CHRISTY." *An updated version of a classical French ski school turn, which is probably the easiest turn to launch in deep snow. Strong upward extension, coupled with forward foot thrust and a lifting of the outside hand, virtually guarantees that you'll turn. A great turn for inexperienced powder skiers just coming to terms with the deep stuff.*

Dancing in the Deep: Perfecting an Effortless Fall-Line Style

Comes the moment when the deep stuff, Rocky Mountain light or California heavy, feels, well, it feels normal, exciting, but no longer strange. You no longer fall every other turn. You seldom lose your balance and head for the trees on one submarining ski with the other one dragging crazily behind you. You're ready for a little pizazz in your powder skiing. And here it comes.

As a first step, you'll need more speed—speed you couldn't possibly have coped with at first. No more starting off from a traverse, even a steep traverse. Drop straight into the fall line and schuss down twenty, thirty, forty feet (depending on the steepness and snow depth) until your skis begin to plane up, actually starting to feel light beneath you. Now, from a normally flexed stance, start pressing the tails of your skis out sideways into the snow, that familiar twisting extension. You start to slow down, feeling the resistance of the snow that you're compressing, as it pushes back up under your feet and skis. At this point, simply relax your legs and *let* that pressure in the snow push your skis, feet and thighs up beneath you. As your skis and legs float up in the snow, turn them toward the fall line and once more start pressing your heels (that is to say, the tails of your skis) out to the other side. That's it. Press and extend to finish a turn, relax and flex to start the next one. The pressing at the finish is the active phase; the relaxing/folding at the start of the turn is almost passive. Resistance from the snow is lifting your thighs and skis while you gently reorient the ski tips downhill. Press to slow down, relax to start again, and repeat, endlessly, down the hill in a cloud of smoking powder, lungs bursting with icy champagne air, a cover photo from *Powder Magazine* come to life. The way it's s'posed to be . . .

At least that's the theory. It will take you a little time to master this pattern—a familiar sequence of effort at the end of one turn, then relaxation to start the next, the same action/reaction, turn and re-turn pattern of dynamic anticipation that we know so well. The key new element here is the use of retraction/extension rather than rising at the start of the turn—but the rest of the pieces were already present. And in my experience there's no clear-cut set of steps, no exercise sequence that will take you from the coping-with-powder level directly to the dancing-through-it peak. Rather, you want to have a pretty clear picture of where you're heading and then simply ski a braver and braver line down the powder as you feel it start to happen. But there are, as usual, a number of little points, insights and tricks that can speed your journey.

For example, speed control is still a problem. You will be gravitating to steeper and steeper slopes, especially in very deep and/or heavier powder. You'll want to slow down with each turn, without however turning your skis so far across the fall line that it becomes difficult to twist them back around into the next turn. Luckily, in powder you're skiing in a three-dimensional snow-filled space, not on a two-dimensional inclined plane, and you can slow yourself considerably just by sinking your ski tails deeper into the snow at the end of each turn. It's the same pressing/extending action we've already discussed, only oriented *vertically downward* into the snow, not totally sideways in a heel-pushing turn. Simply think of grinding or sinking your boot heels deeper into the snow at the end of each turn, which naturally sinks the tails of the skis deeper. I think of "stalling" my forward speed as I sink my tails, then relaxing my legs to let myself plunge down the slope again.

There is a strange similarity between high-level powder dancing and bump skiing. The pressing/extending action at the end of each turn creates a kind of invisible pressure bump under the snow. And this is what pushes your skis and thighs upward when you relax the turning effort—much as the crest of a mogul pushes skis and thighs upward when you hit it. Likewise, you feel poised on an invisible pivot point, skis liberated from the resistance of the snow, ready to be easily turned back toward the fall line with minimal foot action. Nice. As in bump skiing too, arm/hand/pole action is important in powder, establishing a rhythm, synchronizing the phases of the turn. If you forget to reach forward with the new pole you

**FIG. 7.5 FALL-LINE POWDER SKIING WITH
RETRACTION/EXTENSION.** *The way experts ski powder in the
fall line. After a strong finish with twisting extension, the skier
allows the resistance of the deep snow to push legs and skis
back up beneath the body (the relaxation/retraction phase). The
skis are reoriented and reextended in the opposite direction.*

probably won't be ready for the next turn, and you won't make it.

But in the full-on powder boogie, the real fall-line dance, I would say that there's no longer any need for the two tricks I shared with you earlier to achieve a more powerful start to your turn—lifting the outside hand, and pushing or jetting your feet ahead. I keep these two moves in reserve for truly bad, super-heavy, desperate snow conditions. And I only suggested them for the powder neophyte because they virtually guarantee you'll make it around the corner, whether your technique, or your mind, is ready for it or not.

I've already hinted that cut-up, half-powder and half-packed snow is far harder to ski well than the pure untouched deep stuff. Not only is it inconsistent—your skis shoot ahead in the packed patches and then brake violently in piles of loose snow—but it's also tough to know at what moment to give up one's deep snow technique and start skiing it just like the pack. In general, both approaches work. The conservative approach to cut-up, tracked-out semi-powder is to ski a little faster, round out your turns into medium-radius swoopers, and generally stand on both skis just as you would in bottomless deep snow. Weighting both skis here prevents a light inner ski from being caught and knocked aside by big lumps of snow. On the other hand, if you're feeling bold, just about anything works in this in-between snow state.

So when does powder skiing become

easy? How long before the powder paradox dissolves in a cloud of white crystals and you wake in the morning thinking of face-shots in untracked bowls? How long before you skip breakfast to be the first one in the lift line on powder mornings because you know, beyond a shadow of a doubt, that you belong up there, on those virgin slopes, signing your passage with sinuous, sensual first tracks on a blank snowy canvas? How long before you start thinking, talking, dreaming like a powder addict? As I pointed out, skiers blessed with the lightest powder learn faster, while those wrestling with some form of Sierra cement will eventually become more poised and proficient deep-snow skiers. For a strong parallel skier learning to survive, cope with, and actually ski deep snow, albeit in a ho-hum sort of way, it shouldn't take more than a day. Mastery, however, may require a few days or even a few weeks, depending on how friendly the powder is and on how accomplished you already are at linking short turns right down the fall line. A gifted bump skier with little or no experience in powder will make the fastest progress of all.

You'll know you're getting there when you have the strong impression that you are no longer turning your skis through all this extra resistance, but instead, it's the resistance of the snow that is pushing your skis from side to side. You're back in the role of privileged passenger again. You've entered the real powder

FIG. 7.6 ANOTHER VIEW OF ADVANCED POWDER SKIING.
This side view shows the relaxation/retraction phase clearly.
This phase sometimes gives the impression of the skier sitting
back. Beware, it's only an optical illusion.

skier's world: there are no more bad, good and better turns in deep snow, just turns. And from that point on, you'll never, ever find enough powder snow.

- *First things first: develop a stable powder stance with equal weight on both skis.*

- *In light Rocky Mountain fluff, use a spontaneous approach, linking rhythmic fall-line turns on easy to moderate slopes. When the snow gets deeper and steeper, try two purely "powder" tricks: lifting the outside hand/pole, and pushing both feet forward at the start of turns.*

- *In heavier "Sierra cement"–type conditions, begin with the tail of the turn, practicing uphill christies with twisting extension from progressively steeper and steeper traverse lines until you can easily "pull out" of the fall line. Then start complete turns with a rising/lifting motion and foot thrust—the modern "light christy."*

- *Finally, once you can turn in the deep stuff, work on pure fall-line powder technique—relaxation/retraction to start your turns, twisting extension to finish.*

- *In the very steep and deep, sink the tails of your skis vertically into the snow at the end of each turn for more control.*

8

EXTREME DIMENSIONS OF EXPERT SKIING

Faster Speeds, Steeper Slopes, Tougher Snow

Last weekend was perhaps the best two days you ever spent on skis. It snowed and snowed and snowed. Every run, a fresh set of tracks—and what tracks! A real deep-powder festival: effortless, dynamite skiing, runs you'll never forget. And today, looking up from the parking lot, you're surprised to see those white snow flanks on the east face of the mountain are still virgin, miraculously untouched. Not for long, you think, ready for a repeat performance of last week's powder extravaganza. A half-hour later there you stand, poised above a long wave of perfect, trackless snow. Well, almost trackless, no ski tracks anyway, but the wind has been at play here, has etched sand-dune patterns across your blank canvas, and the morning sun is reflecting off some parts of the slope as if they were glass. No matter. It may not be as light and fluffy as last weekend, but you can handle it . . .

Or so you thought.

Your tracks are not a pretty sight. Zigzag lines interspersed with craters. As soon as you push off, your skis are trapped beneath a strange crusty surface, and when you try to turn—forget it! Five hundred feet lower, nursing a bruised ego and a sore ankle, you traverse back around the corner to the packed slope, glad to get out of there in one piece. You understand why no one went out and messed up that sun-baked, wind-scoured face all week; and you're suddenly aware that the mantle of expert skier rests more insecurely on your shoulders than you had thought. It's true . . . every now and then the bubble bursts, the dream of expert skiing dissolves, the poetry vanishes and reality comes back swinging to give you an unexpected drubbing.

Nothing has ever summed up the dream of expert skiing better than the French *toute neige, tout terrain,* which means of course, "all snow, all terrain." Perhaps we could add, to complete this universal description of a skier who is at home anywhere and everywhere, *toute vitesse,* all speeds. The operative word is *all;* not just most snow conditions, or most terrain (as long as it's not too steep), or average speeds—but all of it, any of it, anytime, anywhere. It's an ambitious and inspiring goal. One that can never be realized completely, but whose pursuit will take you way beyond the limits of average skiers.

Testing the limits of your new skills and pushing beyond them is what this chapter is all about. Every skier has limits, even champions, both physical and mental. One of the guiding ideas behind my writing this book was that, generally, it's the lack of specific technical skills, not lack of an expert's mind set, that prevents most skiers from performing at a truly high level. The key breakthrough skills I described in chapters two, three and four—and I've a hunch that with sufficient patience and concentration most of my readers can acquire these skills, indeed have already acquired them by the time they've reached this chapter. But now things change.

As we enter extreme dimensions of expert skiing, as we try to ski right at our limits—or a little beyond—technique alone is no longer enough. One's state of mind becomes critical. Self-confidence, inner calm and alertness, are every bit as important as one's technique. And since almost none of us is born with the courage of a lion or the detached calm of a zen monk, we're going to have to train our minds just as much as our legs and bodies to deal with these extreme conditions. We'll do it with the simplest strategy possible: easing into these demanding conditions—extremely high speeds, extremely steep slopes, and extremely bad snow—one step at a time, upping the ante slowly as we become accustomed to each new skiing environment. Never biting off more than we can chew while we build up new reserves of confidence. In extreme ski conditions, confidence is both crucial to success and a kind of reward for success—the tougher the conditions you manage to ski, the more confidence you gain for even rougher situations.

But confidence is only one half of the mental equation. The other half is good judgment, without which the extreme ski challenges we're about to look at can become dangerous exercises in irresponsible risk-taking. Like the basics of expert skiing, these extreme skills, both mental and physical, can't be learned overnight. If you're tempted, they will take a lot of time, a lot of practice, a lot of crashes. In any domain, progress slows down considerably as you reach your limits.

Is it worth it? You bet. One of the greatest epiphanies in skiing is the moment when you suddenly realize that you can handle it all—when you feel ready, truly ready, for just about anything the mountain may have in store. I would caution you only that the situations we're about to look at are the *final* touches, not at all the basic everyday stuff of expert skiing. You can master such extreme situations only if you already have a very solid command of the basics of high-level skiing. The one-footed stance, early weight shift with a quiet underpivoted initiation, linking turns with dynamic anticipation—all this should be second nature before you consciously go looking for ever higher speeds, steeper slopes, and more and more difficult snow.

Skiing Through Time:
The Challenge of Higher Speeds

High-speed skiing is far from a universal turn on, and I can understand why. One friend of mine, confessing his ambitions to become a super-skier, added the qualifier: "But I don't really want to ski faster than other people, I guess I'm not that macho, I'm only in it for the poetry." I had to applaud his sentiments; I'm not that macho either. I adamantly reject the notion that experts always ski fast or that one must ski at breakneck speeds to qualify as an expert skier. But at some point I always urge my best students to experiment with higher speeds than they're used to, to ski faster than they normally feel is comfortable.

There are a couple of good reasons for this, but the best is for an added dimension of security and safety. No, this is not double talk. Sooner or later, even the most prudent, cautious or just plain timid skiers will, at least momentarily, lose control and find themselves skiing much too fast. You find yourself on a narrow, steep trail and someone falls just ahead of you. You abort that next turn to avoid slamming into the downed skier, pass him in the fall line and just when you've got a clear space to slow down, there's a half-covered stump in your line. So it's abort again, and before you know it you're doing Mach 1— faster than anyone in their right mind would ever ski that trail. At least, faster than *you* would ever ski it. You didn't want to, it just happened. See what I mean? These situations happen. And my point is that if you practice skiing very fast under optimum controlled circumstances, if you develop a certain minimum level of competence and confidence at high-speed skiing, then when something goes wrong and you find yourself tearing down the slope, you will be in control, you'll know what to do—and you'll do it.

There are at least a couple of other reasons to get comfortable with high-speed skiing. One is very curious and concerns the relativity of time, or of our perception of time. It so happens that the faster we move—on skis or off—the slower time seems to pass. Something like speeding up a ciné camera to obtain slow-motion film. Of course initially it's all a blur, but as you tune in to high-speed skiing, you seem to have more and more time to focus on and appreciate everything that's happening around you. A real treat. And there's a bonus. I'm going to suggest that you practice high-speed skiing on safe, moderate slopes with good runouts, where you won't get psyched-out. But if, after even a short séance of skiing very fast, you then head for some really tough slopes, very steep or bumpy, and ski them at normal speeds, you'll get the impression of having far more time than you need to prepare for that next bump, that next turn—and you'll handle those challenges better than ever.

Finally, of course, the obvious reason: skiing fast is fun. Another one of those almost surreal, almost out-of-body experiences that expert skiing offers. Speed itself is not scary. What makes us nervous is not knowing how to handle it—and the consequent anxiety about what *might* happen to us. That old story: fear of the unknown. And I propose we eliminate it in a couple of easy steps.

But first, having convinced you (I hope) that skiing fast might be a good thing, we should answer the question: Just how fast is fast? It's purely a psychological matter. Fast is simply anything faster than what you're used to. Cautious beginners typically ski around 5 mph or less (hard to believe it's that slow); intermediate skiers feel very comfortable in the 10 mph range; while for strong skiers speeds in the 15 to 20 mph range are already fast, and at 25 mph you're wailing like a banshee! Yet I find a 10 mph schuss on skinny cross-country racing skis to be a hair-raising experience. It's truly relative.

Skiers are often influenced by the knowledge that top racers can hit 60 or 70 mph in a downhill course, and tend to assume that just because something felt fast they too were doing around 50. No way! Downhill racing speeds are an altogether different world, requiring special skis, equipment, helmets, specially prepared race courses, and above all, years of specialized training. Our own world is different, but not necessarily less exciting. You'll get more than your share of thrills and chills by notching up your personal speedometer 30, 40 or 50 percent, without ever approaching the speeds attained in downhill competition, or taking those risks.

Our game plan is simple: just start by schussing straight more often. Most steep slopes end in a runout of some sort, so I would ask you not to ski the last few turns down to the flat but take it straight. At first only the last couple of turns, then progressively more and more. And you can also start schussing very easy slopes, greens and the odd blue, where you might normally make graceful and lazy (but not necessary) show-off turns. Take care only that you're schussing toward easier terrain, not into a mine field of new bumps or other problems. And please note I'm not suggesting that you just go up the mountain one day and try skiing everything twice as fast: start with small stretches of extra-fast skiing—where you can see there's no trouble ahead, no blind corners, no bodies to avoid, no sudden stops. In fact, no sudden anything!

The key strategy to skiing very fast is that you, the skier, must paradoxically move very slowly. I always explain this by an analogy with driving a car. At 5 mph in first gear, in a shopping center parking lot for example, it's okay to spin the steering wheel or to slam on the brakes. But either of those actions at 60 mph on the freeway would cause your automobile to go careening out of control, a potential disaster. Likewise with skiing very fast. If you have to slow down and stop, you must do so gently, slowly, progressively—just as you put a gentle, almost imperceptible pressure on the brake pedal when slowing your car from high freeway speeds.

You'll find that the tiniest actions suffice at high speeds. Miniature steering efforts with the foot are all it takes to ease your skis into long swooping arcs. And it goes without saying that all high-speed turns are more or less long-radius arcs. Short turns, like jerky movements, are verboten at high speeds. So pick some friendly terrain, build up a big head of steam, and try a couple of long, gentle, high-speed turns to a stop—just to see how little effort, and how much patience, it takes.

Now for some serious high-speed cruising on freshly groomed green and blue slopes, without a lot of skiers on them. When you're looking for speed, I'd recommend being first up the mountain and skiing like hell from 9 to 10 in the morning before the daily crowds arrive—and never pushing for speed in the late afternoon when masses of tired skiers are clogging the main runs back to the area base.

A couple of details: When skiing fast, your arms will be critical for small balance adjustments—carry them wider than normal, always ahead of your hips. Maintain your one-footed stance exclusively—on the downhill ski when traversing or on the outside ski of the turn—except for moments when you're really schussing straight down the fall line when it's best to stand on two feet. And avoid any forward pressure in your boots that will make the skis want to turn too much, too fast, with too much skidding. At high speeds it's best to remain flat-footed or *slightly* on your heels.

In reality, there are almost no unique technical adaptations to high-speed skiing except the all-important one of making yourself act, and react, very slowly. You must train yourself not to overreact to anything and this in turn means looking, and thinking, ahead, way

ahead, down the slope. You can't afford to put yourself in a position where extra speed becomes excessive speed, and you wind up injuring yourself or, worse yet, someone else. You also have to stay much farther away from other skiers than you would at more normal speeds. Not only to avoid disastrous collisions, but just as important, to avoid psyching-out weaker skiers and ruining their day on the slopes. As an instructor I'm particularly aware of the jitters experienced by a lot of novices when hot shots flash by in their peripheral vision; it's devastating. And it's all too common. Especially since the best slopes for cruising at really high speeds are groomed, easy runs, not double black diamonds—just the sort of terrain where you're likely to encounter insecure novices. So be a sport. You don't have to barely avoid a near-collision with someone to shake him up; it's enough to ski past him too closely. High-speed skiers should be so discreet that nobody is even aware that they've just shot down a slope at three times the usual velocity. Do it right.

And a note on the natural progression of high-speed skiing: I've suggested that you begin with short stretches, sections rather than whole runs—at first simply schussing more and more—and then train yourself to make long, calm, progressive, high-speed turns. One moves next to continuous, nonstop runs on moderate groomed slopes. I sometimes like to challenge my students, and myself, to ski an entire slope with only X number of turns—say only five big turns on a slope where normally you'd do dozens. Even the biggest, fastest arcs still have a valuable speed control function. Remember to stay in your arc until your exit speed from the turn is about the same as the speed you carried into it. Accelerating madly through a series of uncompleted half-turns is not my idea of expert skiing. Speed alone is not the goal. If it were, you'd take every hill straight, and you wouldn't last long. Control, poise and finesse at high speeds is more like it. And finally, once you've become skilled at high-speed cruising on groomed slopes, you'll be better prepared for skiing fast on rougher terrain—through small to medium rolling bumps, for example.

Big fast sweeping turns—often referred to as "GS turns" because they resemble a giant slalom—through even gentle bumps are quite a trip! You should feel your way into this sort of skiing prudently, though. It's even more demanding, physically and technically, than classical short-turn, fall-line mogul skiing—which is why so few skiers, except for top racers, ever really exercise this option in bumps. But you can ease into it by learning to ski straight across gentle bumps at high speed, before trying to turn through them. In such situations, a real expert's skis will hug the terrain, snaking up and down over the surface of the bumps, seemingly with no shocks and no unintentional air time. The secret: our old friend, the one-footed stance. The problem with standing on both legs when cruising fast over bumps is that the two legs together are just too strong;

they resist the compression of each bump instead of collapsing with it; and the "two-footed" skier gets bashed about quite a bit. Conversely, if you're riding through the bumps exclusively on one ski, then that downhill leg which is already a bit fatigued from supporting your whole weight will "collapse" in perfect synchronization with every bump you encounter. But don't just believe me. Test it yourself by alternating several fast traverses straight across a mogul field, some on two feet, some on only the downhill ski—you'll be shocked and delighted at the difference.

Enough hints for now on skiing fast. Better to practice high-speed skiing comfortably and safely on your own than to let yourself be egged into it by crazy "go-for-it" friends. It's a mental discipline, remember, skiing through time as much as space, and far more abstract than our next challenge, very steep slopes.

Fear of Falling: Skiing on Extremely Steep Slopes

Many skiers will never face this challenge, because there aren't many steep slopes left. Let me explain. The mountains haven't gotten any flatter. But at most ski areas nowadays steep slopes turn into mogul runs, which don't feel nearly as steep because of the flat tops of each bump, and which don't demand the same technique as steep, smooth slopes. That's what we're really talking about here: steep and smooth. Walls of snow. Vertiginous cliffs of snow.

This sort of experts-only skiing, although

rare, is definitely alive and well, particularly on the biggest, wildest western mountains like Mammoth, Jackson Hole and Squaw, to name only a few. Such big mountains have more steep terrain than the operators can groom, or the hordes can pack and scrape into moguls. In winter, mountain winds funnel loose snow up isolated faces and chutes forming a fantastic solid but not too hard surface of wind-blasted powder. In spring, alternate freezing and melting transform these same faces and chutes into smooth walls of corn snow—sheet ice in the morning thawing to a perfect resilient velvet by midday. These are skiers' dream surfaces, but tilted at such an angle that you don't want to even think about falling. Even hard-core heroes hesitate and breathe deeply before committing themselves here.

The technique for taming such steep, smooth faces of snow is known as *shortswing* (sometimes "braking shortswing") and basically consists of linked short turns punctuated by vigorous edgesets that help slow the descent as well as bouncing, or rebounding, the skier into the next turn. Shortswing used to be more widely practiced, more visible on the slopes, but has tended to go a bit out of fashion in this age of carving smooth arcs, of absorbing mean moguls. Still, nothing has replaced it for dealing with steep, smooth, hard slopes.

And I should say here, as an aside, that although skiing is constantly evolving and changing, almost nothing has ever been definitively discarded. Sometimes techniques have been shelved and almost forgotten for a few years, or a few generations, but invariably they show up again in certain special contexts. The absurdly old-fashioned heel-thrusting of the official Austrian Ski School technique of the 1960s has disappeared from the slopes— but the same heel thrust is still valuable in deep-powder skiing, and indispensable in heavy "death-snow" crud as we'll soon see. The telemark turn, a strange maneuver indeed, possible only with free-heel, cross-country equipment, was given up for dead by Alpine skiers in Europe and the States after World War I. But it was rediscovered by young athletes in Crested Butte, Colorado, around a decade ago, and today the telemark is experiencing a renaissance of popularity among hot young skiers in the Rockies (but that's another story and perhaps, one of these days, another book). Likewise, nothing has come along that works better than classical short-swing for dealing with extra-steep slopes.

There is also, I may as well confess, one extreme level of steep skiing beyond what can be handled with shortswing. Indeed, this tiny subworld of the sport is commonly called *extreme skiing,* and represents a halfway step between skiing and alpinism, where the skills of both sports are needed merely to survive. Extreme skiing is well known, if not widely popular, in the Alps. Its practitioners routinely compete to make "first descents" of snow faces and couloirs that were heretofore the exclusive province of the mountaineer, armed with ice ax and crampons. Generally, extreme skiing starts on slopes of around 45 degrees (to my knowledge, no named run at any ski area is over 40 degrees, and even slopes of 35 degrees are frighteningly steep). But another way of defining extreme skiing might be that while on the super-steep a fall is always very serious, in extreme skiing it could be fatal. Needless to say, I don't want to encourage anyone to go out and risk his or her life on one successful turn—so we'll ignore this rarefied branch of the sport and concentrate on the ordinary garden-variety of heart-stopping steepness. For ultimate extreme skiing you use a special turn that the French call a *virage sauté-pédalé,* which is just as hard to do as it is to pronounce or translate. I've covered this turn in detail in my earlier book, *Backcountry Skiing,* for the handful of folks ready—and crazy enough—to try it. But for the steepest skiing that a reasonable, brave human being might want to do, pure shortswing is all you need.

Radical shortswing on the steeps is a complex movement pattern. I'll try first to paint a global picture of these turns, then offer you a step-by-step practice sequence to learn, master and apply. Shortswing on very steep slopes works like this:

With a totally anticipated upper body position, the skier sideslips a few feet down the slope, then simultaneously plants his downhill pole and rapidly edges his skies with an inward push of knees and ankles. This is the so-called edgeset, and when done rapidly it not only stops the skier's sliding, but also creates a reaction or rebound that bounces the skier's feet and legs right off the snow. Momentarily airborne, he supports himself solidly on that downhill pole while quickly pivoting both skis in the air, to the fall line or even a bit beyond—on the super-steep the last thing you want to do is linger lazily in the fall line gathering momentum. And upon landing, the skier *sideslips* both skis rapidly around to the horizontal where the process is repeated. Note the emphasis on sideslipping. This is the exact opposite of a carved round arc. The tracks of radical shortswing are more like a succession of skidded fish-hook shapes. The skidding allows both a very short turn and maximum braking action. Extreme steepness and speed don't mix well.

Knowing what shortswing is, and doing it, are two different things—and doing it so well that you *know* it's going to work on the steepest, scariest slopes is something else again. For reasons of simple survival, it's imperative to have the pattern drilled into legs and body long before you have to depend on it for serious steep terrain. Here's how we're going to make shortswing an acquired habit:

Start with the key new element—edgeset and rebound—which isn't much used in everyday skiing. On a practice pitch, steep and smooth, but short and totally nonthreatening, I'd like you to try sideslipping to a strong edge-

FIG. 8.2 SHORTSWING WITH EDGESET AND REBOUND. Still the best technique for slopes of extreme steepness. The skier skids to a rapid, powerful edgeset, rebounds into the air to turn the skis, and skids to a new edgeset. Maximum anticipation.

set. Slip down a few feet in a very anticipated position and, wham, slam those edges into the slope with a sharp snap of knees and lower leg. Just as you hit your edges, plant your lower pole well below your boots. And then? At first you won't experience much rebound, so aid nature with a short explosive hop from the low, compressed position of your edgeset. We're only looking for synchronization of the three elements—edgeset, pole plant, and an upward reaction—not real power.

Next, repeat the process diagonally across your steep practice pitch—traversing, side-slipping to an edgeset/poleplant, then re-bounding/hopping your skis back into their original traversing direction, and repeat. You've recognized that this sideslipping to an edgeset is just another form of our familiar preturn. This sequence across the slope is a classic "garland" exercise, as old and as old-fashioned as shortswing itself, but still unsur-passed for training your body to perform this one critical maneuver—the edgeset/rebound you'll need on extremely steep slopes. After sliding your skis down the slope to an edgeset, then popping back up off the snow several times, simply turn your skis a bit farther in the air, land in a full turn and repeat this sideslip/edgeset sequence in the other direction. Do it. Don't hesitate. Ten minutes of this simple, almost boring exercise and you'll have ac-quired a vital new element for skiing the steep.

Now put your edgeset to use, at first on smooth but not terribly steep pitches, and then, progressively, on steeper and steeper slopes. If you're looking only for open slots long enough for five or six turns, it's amazing what truly steep walls of snow you can find at even modest ski areas. (Of course, by the time you're ready to ski *Huevos,* or *Philippe's* at Mammoth, you'd better be prepared for thirty or forty perfect fall-line, shortswing turns in a row.) The turns you're aiming for now are short-radius, fast-pivoting and continuous. The edgeset at the end of each turn produces the reaction, the bounce that lifts you into the next turn. In essence these are turns without a middle, without an arc or "belly." A dynamic rebounded initiation leads immediately to a rapid skid to a new edgeset. The skis move quickly from one horizontal position to the opposing horizontal position. The feeling is sharp, snappy, aggressive—not loose and flowing. To develop this turn, simply start with the kind of short linked, fall-line turns you already do (you are, after all, a very strong skier by now) and progressively emphasize the edgeset/rebound effect between turns.

Here are a few more tips that can help considerably as you slowly increase the pitch of your "comfort zone" steeper and steeper and steeper. During the initiation phase when your skis rebound off the snow from their edgeset, try to retract your heels a bit beneath you. This will lift the tails of the skis more parallel to the true angle of the hill, so they won't snag on even the steepest slopes.

Turn fast! Super-steep slopes may be the

one place in expert skiing where it's a good thing to rush your turn. The steeper the slope, the farther you want to pivot your skis in the air. If you're totally anticipated—body, shoulders and hips aimed straight downhill—it should be easy to twist your skis right around to the fall line and, with a little extra effort, beyond. Land predominantly on your outside foot—as smoothly as you can, given the sense of crisis that tends to accompany turning on a very steep slope—and don't try to "dig in" with your edges until your skis have skidded rapidly to the horizontal.

On very steep slopes you will, in fact, have the sensation of falling rather than skiing between edgesets. It's a wild feeling—do your best to enjoy it. In such cases it may take an extra moment, and a few extra feet of skidding, before your attempt to set the edges stops this "fall."

Finally, because shortswing is often needed in tight, constricted situations (narrow snow chutes, for instance, or rock-lined couloirs), you'll want to slide straight down the fall line in the last phase of the turn rather than carving forward (i.e., across the hill). The trick to realizing this straight-down style of descent is landing from your rebounded pivot with your weight on the *heel* of your outside foot. Weight on the ball of the foot tends to make the skis track forward across the slope, and if it's a narrow gully, look out!

So, after a certain amount of creative practice (it's usually possible, with enough imagination, to find steep, smooth slopes *some-where* at a ski area), you've now got a pretty fair version of classical shortswing. A turn that seems to work fine on steep practice slopes. But life on the steep is not quite the same as on a practice slope. Ultimately, you'll want to find some serious, long, steep walls of snow to test yourself on. Skiing the very steep is always a kind of test; no one does it for relaxation.

You'll find the difficulty of launching a series of shortswing turns to be directly proportional to the size and steepness of the slope beneath you. And you'll also find that getting started is the hardest part. Invariably, once you pass from ordinary to extraordinary steepness, that first turn takes a major effort of will. A little mental rehearsal, on the brink, may help—but too much thinking about it will only psych you out. Far better to remember our preturn strategy, for that is exactly what the initial sideslip to an edgeset is. If needed, sideslip down a few feet to a strong edgeset, and then repeat this sideslip/edgeset a couple of times —just to get used to the steepness, the snow surface and the sort of balance it demands— before actually turning downhill. If you're perched on the steep, clinging to the slope with your edges, and you try to launch your first turn from a standstill, or from a timid forward traversing action, you'll be in big trouble. The preturn pattern of sideslipping to an edgeset before your first turn is a guarantee of success, an effective way of fooling your body into behaving as if it was already in the middle of an active sequence of turns.

And finally, don't merely use your poles, *over*use them. They are your outriggers and your balance props on the super-steep—a few supplementary poleplants per turn with that outside hand can do wonders for your stability.

It's an incredible feeling: Butterflies in the stomach, a quick gulp or two of cold air, the first critical edgeset and suddenly—having survived one turn on a slope that's patently too steep for reasonable people to want to ski—suddenly it's not just shortswing, it's an adventure! It's precisely because you don't belong there (nobody does) that skiing extremely steep walls of snow is such a thrill. A kind of real-life ballet of the absurd on skis. An overwhelming adrenaline rush. Here, too, time and perceptions slow and change. You fall forever from one turn to the next; you hear your skis scraping to an edgeset from a long, long way off; you look down at the tiny figures of skiers below you as if they were dwellers on another planet. And your skis continue to edgeset, rebound, pivot in the air and slide to a new edgeset, again and again, the clockwork dance of the steep, punctuated by powerful pole plants, deep breathing. The one thing you don't, shouldn't, mustn't, can't think about is . . . falling.

At least, you shouldn't think about falling while you're out there on those snowy cliffs, doing it. But you should take the consequences of falling on steep slopes very seriously. I've seen people topple hundreds and hundreds of feet, narrowly escaping rocks and trees or, unfortunately, not escaping them. And I've often skied super-steep slopes where a fall would be unthinkable. But I have thought about it. And you should too. If you're flying on faith and guts instead of judgment and skill, sooner or later you'll crash.

What I suggest is simply this: Take your ski adventures on steep slopes very seriously. Above all, practice your basic shortswing technique so long and hard that the moves are totally automatic before you get out on a frozen steep wall of snow where mistakes might be unhealthy. Some people can master this skiing pattern in a couple of sessions, others (who can also be very fine skiers) may need a whole season's shortswing practice before they trust themselves on the truly steep. Don't push your limits with cliffs or nasty obstacles below you. And be sure you're brave enough to chicken out, and come back another day if you really don't feel ready for a given slope.

Finally, should you fall on an unthinkably steep slope, it's sometimes possible to use a ski-pole self-arrest. For this you'll need to have taken your hands out of your pole straps before starting. You simply slide both hands very close to the basket of one pole, having dropped the other—and slowly, ever so slowly, dig the tip of the pole into the snow, leaning on it, until it brings you to a stop. I've saved myself about twice in twenty years with this nifty maneuver. But it's basically a last resort. Real security on the super-steep comes only from good judgment, from hours and hours of patient skiing drill, from slowly jacking up the challenge one notch at a time as your skill on the steep increases, instead of getting out there over your head. Skiing the super-steep is a great adventure for expert skiers, which real experts do not take lightly.

And as I said at the beginning, not many ski areas offer this sort of challenge; when steep slopes become moguled, you ski the moguls, period. So you may become a super-skier and ski at a very high level for years and years without ever facing the challenge of the steep. Not so with truly awful snow. Snow is the sine qua non of the skiing experience, and some mighty weird white stuff can fall down from the sky, just about anywhere.

From Bad to Worse: Skiing in Terrible Conditions

I've been known to say that there's no such thing as bad snow, only bad skiers—and I'm not sure whether that's a bad joke or a terrible lie. Over the years, I've seen a lot of pretty abominable snow conditions, and I'm sure you have too, at least on occasion. To be honest, I respond to the challenge of skiing in lousy conditions. There are probably days when sensible skiers, even great ones, are better off staying in the lodge. But I came to skiing with a mountaineering background; and one of my early goals was to be able to wander off into the high backcountry in winter, far from groomed slopes, lifts and ski patrollers. I quickly discovered that I had to be able to ski everything—the good (powder and corn), the bad (breakable crust and windslab), and the ugly (heavy rotten spring slush)—the works! I also discovered the delight of coming to terms with the very worst snow conditions. Not falling in love with bad snow, but deriving a lot of satisfaction from being able to turn and enjoy myself where others could only swear and fall. This almost perverse passion for bad snow has taught me a lot of specialized tricks that I enjoy sharing with like-minded skiers.

For me there are two main sorts of truly terrible snow conditions. The first is a predominantly springtime horror that doesn't really have an exact name. I'm talking about very wet, soggy, deep, rotten snow—maybe we could call it glop—which is certainly more likely in the Far West and Pacific Northwest, but can actually occur almost anywhere, in the Rockies, and certainly in the Alps. The second main type of "death snow" is so-called breakable crust. Usually formed by the sun's action, melting and refreezing the surface, but sometimes by wind, breakable crust can occur any time during the season. It's an off-piste phenomenon that you only run across when skiing away from packed runs. Both these types of snow can stop good skiers cold. Or break their legs.

At Mammoth Mountain during the annual ski instructors' exams, I've seen wet overnight spring dumps that ressembled thick layers of Elmer's Glue—and in which only a handful of the over two hundred assembled ski instructors were able to make more than two turns without falling. And I must say, too, that I've seen snow conditions so tough and dangerous that I wouldn't encourage anyone to ski them—students, friends, even other instructors—out of an awareness that only perfectly functioning release bindings would keep their legs intact (and nothing's perfect). So don't take this discussion as an invitation or encouragement to go out and do something dumb. Yet I know I'm writing this book for ambitious skiers, folks who want to enlarge, explore and test their limits. And someday you'll find yourself wrestling with almost unskiable snow. Here, then, are the best strategies I know for dealing with the sort of bad snow that probably shouldn't be skied at all.

To turn in the deepest, rottenest glop, I suggest a very awkward but powerful turn that I've nicknamed my "Austrian power turn" because it ressembles an exaggerated caricature of the heel-thrusting official style of the Austrian National Ski School in former years. We're going to take two elements that I suggested in the last chapter for creating more powerful turns in heavy, deep powder—the forward thrust of both feet to start and the sideways twisting extension of the tails to finish—and exaggerate the hell out of them!

Like this: Start your turn by sinking so low that you're almost sitting on your heels, anticipated as always, and as you plant your downhill pole, launch a very powerful extension. But instead of just extending upward from this extra-low position I want you to extend your legs out from beneath you—pushing both feet forward, down the hill, into the new turn. And you can add that powerful lifting action of the outside hand and pole at the same time. Logic tells you that such a start to a turn will put you in a hopelessly sitting back position. But it doesn't happen, because the sort of death snow we're considering is so heavy that it slows the forward push of your skis enough for your body to catch up. This is an incredibly powerful initiation that will launch a turn even in pure wet cement. To keep such a turn going, just change your forward foot thrust to a strong sideways extension, driving your heels away from you through the glop.

There's a tremendous flaw in these turns. It's nearly impossible to link them rhythmically together, since at the end of each one you have to sink down low again to prepare the next forward leg extension. But what the hell! This comical Austrian power turn is merely a secret weapon that you can dust off and use when all else fails, when no other turn works. It's not an elegant or efficient way of skiing, but I guarantee that this baby will get you around.

Breakable crust is a far more subtle challenge—particularly a variable crust that sometimes supports you and sometimes breaks, dropping your skis into the soft snow beneath but trapping your legs in the hard crust. Ugh! The first step in skiing any such crusty snow surface is to abandon the one-footed stance and *distribute your weight absolutely evenly across both skis.* A crust that will shatter under one ski bearing all your weight may perhaps support two skis, each bearing half your weight. You should smooth out all your movements and ski with the utmost delicacy—no sudden jerky moves. A little extra smoothness can also keep the crust from breaking under you. Often the lightest and subtlest skiers can ski comfortably on top of a fragile crust as though it were hardpack, while bigger and more brutal folk crash through on each turn. But sometimes no amount of subtlety helps, and you can't will yourself to weigh half what you really do. Then it's time to abandon delicate moves and ski with real power.

Follow this general strategy. In breakable crust ski fairly slowly, using continuous short turns and no traverses. You don't want to find yourself accelerating in a long traverse with your skis trapped beneath the crust, and continuous, linked turns will keep your speed down. A fall at slow speeds is a lot safer—and you'll take a lot of falls before taming breakable crust. For the same reason, hold your skis tightly together and keep them that way. A fall in this position is safer than a fall with one ski under the crust and one above, or with each ski going in different directions. For turning, your best bet is to start with a lifting/retraction movement of both legs—like absorption in big bumps—that will pull your ski tips momentarily out of the crust. And then, having freed and twisted your two skis in the new direction, press them solidly back through the crust, slamming and breaking it with the tails. Tough, brutal skiing, but it can work.

What I've just described is a general strategy, not a real learning sequence. There is none. You simply have to go out and thrash around in the stuff. These suggestions are only guideposts. If the crust is so weird that all your efforts at launching reasonably normal short turns with a retraction/lifting of the legs fail, there's nothing left but to "leap and land."

The leap-and-land strategy is simplicity itself. With almost no forward speed, and with whatever support you can get from a pole plant, simply jump both skis out of the snow, turn them clear through the fall line in the air, and land back in the crust with the turn completed. Once you break through upon landing, you're not going anywhere—for better or worse, the turn's over. Leap and land, when nothing else works. It's bloody hard work, and produces the most inelegant series of zigzag tracks; but it will get you down almost anything. And you'll have great stories to tell in the bar about the unbelievable junk you skied through.

A last thought on ugly snow conditions. It's always a matter of degree. There are slightly crusted slopes and impossibly crusted ones; there is heavy wet glop, and bottomless rotten glop. Some bad snow is better, some worse. So how do you know what your dealing with? The best way to test the water without diving in over your head is to use your trusty preturn. Say you're standing just outside the ski-area ropes, looking into a sun-baked bowl of trackless snow, and a sixth sense tell you: Watch it, this may be death snow! Don't simply commit blindly to the first turn. Think of your preturn as a preview of what's to come. If you have trouble steering the positive uphill arc of your preturn, then you know you'll have even more trouble turning downhill. In any case, however tricky or challenging the snow, the initial preturn gives you a moment to adjust your balance and adapt your movements, before the moment of truth. If the preturn flat-out doesn't work, it may be time to turn around and hike back to the packed slopes. The real secret of skiing terribly difficult conditions is knowing when you're ready, and admitting it when you're not. This sort of challenge will still be there next weekend, or next season.

And indeed, no matter how comfortable you become skiing one or another sort of extreme condition, there will always be some new challenge waiting—if you're looking for challenges, that is. Consider jumping, for example: Jumping in mogul fields, jumping off cornices, hair jumps off concave berms of snow, real organized springtime geländejumping contests where skiers sail over a hundred feet in the air. Jumping is a challenge for sure. I'm not planning to say much about jumping for the simple reason that while it's easy to jump on skis, it's fairly hard to land right. And dangerous to land wrong. A number of my friends, gifted professional skiers, have blown out their knees and ended full-time skiing careers by landing wrong from reasonably simple jumps. In my view, jumping is probably a good deal riskier than skiing in breakable crust. But it's also a legitimate, exciting, sometimes irresistible skiing challenge; a real thrill. One more potential dimension of expert skiing and occasionally, when speed and the shape of the hill conspire to send the jumper into orbit, an extreme dimension indeed.

For those of you who are as tempted and attracted by air time as snow time, I offer only one important piece of advice. Watch your landings. Avoid flat landings like the plague; they hurt. Look for steep-pitched landings; and as you come down, try to keep your skis parallel to the landing slope, dropping the tips and/or pulling up the tails. The smoother your reentries, the longer you can keep on jumping and enjoying it. Since my knees have been somewhat brutalized from a number of sports accidents, I tend to avoid air time on skis—with the exception, that is, of cornice jumping onto steep fields of forgiving, cushioning deep powder. Ahhhh!

There are other extreme dimensions, other challenges for expert skiers, and always will be. You'll find your own, some of which I've barely hinted at, or missed altogether. After all, I didn't set out to write this book as an encyclopedia of expert skiing, but as a springboard to launch average skiers into the expert's world. I think we've come a long way together. It's *your* turn now.

- *The faster you ski, the slower your movements must be. Braking, stopping and turning are all gradual and progressive moves at very high speeds.*

- *Shortswing—a turn for extreme steeps: edgeset and rebound to start; rapid pivoting in the air; quick skidded turn to a new edgeset with total anticipation.*

- *In heavy rotten snow, try the "Austrian power turn." From an ultra-low position, start with exaggerated forward extension of the legs; finish with twisting extension.*

- *In breakable crust—equal weighting; linked short turns to keep speed down; start turns with a lifting/retraction of the legs.*

- *In death snow when all else fails—leap and land!*

9

FLAG FEVER

The Racing Game

We've all been there—poised in the starting gate. Whether we belonged there or not, in real life or merely, Walter Mitty-like, in our imaginations after watching an Olympic performance on the tube. The race course below, an incomprehensible forest of bright-colored flags. Breathing hard, knuckles wrapped tight around the pole grips, ready to shove off. The starter's voice, "Racer ready . . . set . . . go!" And the rest, usually, an multicolored blur: a paradoxical combination of the flags coming at you too fast to sort out, while despite your best efforts, you ski down the course too slowly. The relief of crossing the finish, an enormous dashing stop christy and then the sobering, distinctly unromantic information provided by the electronic stopwatch: so many seconds, so many tenths, hundredths or thousandths—never quite as fast as it felt, never quite fast enough . . .

Racing is not merely another aspect of expert skiing, it's a whole separate world. Far more books have been written about ski racing than about advanced or expert skiing. Many more specialized coaching programs and racing camps exist than intensive instructional programs designed to produce all-around expert skiers. Clearly enough, ski racing is not what this book is about. Why, then, this chapter?

One reason is that almost all skiers will have at least some casual contact with the world of ski racing. And a more important reason is that racing, even occasional and totally nonserious racing, so-called recreational racing, is a superb discipline, a kind of ultimate technical game. The discipline comes from the total lack of choice once you're launched down a race course: you have to turn where the gates, poles or flags are set, not where you want to. (Of course, much the same can be said about fall-line bump skiing.) Perhaps the ultimate value of racing as a technical ski game is tied directly to the feedback you receive every time you go down a course: Is this tricky combination, this abrupt right turn, easier this time or harder? Are you skidding too low to make the next gate easily, or do you have plenty of time to set up? Even without a coach, without recorded times, skiing through a race course tells you a lot—more than you sometimes want to know—about the state of your ski technique.

Any racing, a little or a lot, will contribute mightily to your progress and development as an expert skier. This holds true even for skiers, like myself, who are resolutely uncompetitive, who totally lack that killer instinct which drives born competitors past their normal limits in race situations. So even if you have no natural interest in ski racing, I would suggest that you have everything to gain and nothing to lose by participating, from time to time, in some sort of recreational or "fun" racing of which the widespread NASTAR program is the perfect example.

Secrets of a NASTAR Gold:
Success in Recreational Racing

NASTAR, which stands for National Standard Race, is a simplified ski-racing program that exists at over one hundred and thirty ski areas across the United States. The course is a series of alternate green and blue giant slalom flags (one banner stretched between two poles). This type of course is referred to as a single-pole course, in which the skier simply makes a turn around every flag. It totally eliminates the complex route-finding required in traditional "amateur" slalom and giant-slalom courses in which the skier must pass between pairs of pole, called gates, that are occasionally set in bewildering and labyrinthine patterns—at least for the neophyte. Anyone can get through a NASTAR course, even novice skiers. The trick is to get through the course fast.

Even more intriguing is the pacesetter/handicap system. A gifted racer, the pacesetter, who has been ranked against other pacesetters at national time trials, opens the course and establishes a time against which all the other participants' times are compared. A handicap system based on age and sex ranks the participants according to how close they come to the pacesetter's time. And medals—bronze, silver and gold—are awarded if one can come within a certain percentage of the pacesetter's time. Strong skiers have little problem obtaining a bronze NASTAR medal after a couple of tries. A silver medal is something to be proud of, and very few skiers indeed manage the speed necessary to qualify for a gold NASTAR pin.

Yet an amazing number of instructors are able to qualify for the NASTAR gold, without being either serious or talented racers. They do it not by *racing* the course well but by *skiing* it well. And what I propose to share with you now are the few strategies and tips you'll need to do the same thing—ski a NASTAR course precisely and efficiently, and eventually get your gold!

As our point of departure I want you to realize that a fast time in a race course depends on two factors. The first, how fast you can ski, seems obvious. But the second, how well you avoid the various errors that can slow you down, is much more important. There are very few ways that a skier can speed up—but the little errors and screw-ups that cost you seconds are legion. So our overall strategy will be to ski a clean, efficient line that avoids any unnecessary deceleration, rather than to rush down the NASTAR course pell-mell looking for extra speed. Poling like a madman between gates, for example, may feel very dynamic, as though you're really "going for it," but all it usually does is unbalance you and make it harder to start the next turn on time and guide it without excess skidding.

The first prerequisite for that NASTAR gold we want is, of course, a clean, efficient expert turn. The sort of turn we learned to make in chapters two and three, with a bit of the carving skills discussed in chapter six thrown in for good measure. A turn initiated with early weight transfer to the top ski and a minimum of leg twisting action; then controlled in a more or less carved arc with the skier solidly balanced on the edge of his or her outside foot. Skiers who are still riding both skis through the arc of their turns will be lucky to qualify for a bronze in a NASTAR race because their skis will be skidding sideways on each turn. But an efficient turn is just the beginning. The real question is: *Where to turn?*

At least ninety percent of the skiers who try NASTAR and other fun races turn too late. By that I mean that they wait until they get to the pole (or poles) which they're supposed to turn around, before they begin the turning movement. The result is always the same: trying to get around the corner at the last minute, they overpivot their skis and skid sideways, dropping way below the best line to the next pole. They end up so low that they are traversing across to that next pole almost horizontally instead of racing down on it from above. So, as a general rule, I want you to start your turns *way before the pole*. Start early enough so that you've already finished your turn as you pass the pole. That's right: as you pass each pole you should already be lined up, aimed for the next one. This means not turning just a little bit earlier, but turning a whole lot earlier.

It may not sound natural, but it works. To prove my point I want you to take a close look at the next NASTAR race course you see. If possible, get there early enough to see the pace-setter run, or else concentrate on where the very best skiers are turning, and compare their line to the tracks left by the majority of the racers. The difference is striking. While most skiers turn after passing the poles, the best racers have always completed their turn by the time they pass the pole! You can too; it's only a question of timing. And you'll be turning on better snow instead of fighting the chatter marks left by the majority of racers who are edging like mad (and in vain) trying to stop their sideways skid below the pole.

It's always a challenge to think clearly in a race course. Flag fever does that. And it's patently impossible to concentrate on more than one thought as you rush from gate to gate. So your racing mantra will be simple: *Turn early! Turn early! Turn early!* Keep after it until it becomes second nature to step onto that top ski long before you reach the pole. Your NASTAR times will improve dramatically. But we're not finished yet.

You can also improve your turn, making it more of a racing than a cruising turn. Instead of merely shifting your weight to the top ski, you can step it, skate it, or simply place it out to the side at a better angle to enter the turn. The idea behind such a start is simple. The

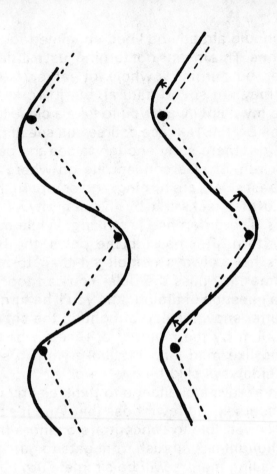

FIG. 9.1 SLOW AND FAST LINES IN A NASTAR COURSE. On the left, the slow path of an inexperienced racer: Turns are started at the last minute as the skier passes the pole; as a result, the skier skids too low and must traverse back to the next pole at a shallow, slow angle. On the right, the track of a more experienced racer: Turns are started early, with a lateral step that gives the racer enough room to clear the pole, yet still follow a steeper, faster line between poles.

fastest line down the course would be one with your skis always aimed directly at the next pole. But this line could bring you so close to that pole that there would be no room to maneuver and start your next turn; so it's tempting to ski more across the hill, which will bring you higher above the pole and thus give you more room—but that's a slower line. The answer: ski the steepest, fastest possible line between turns and at the last second, as you're about to launch your turn, step your top ski a little higher up the slope to gain the needed room. So much for theory. It's a good theory and the exaggerated step shows up in ski-racing technique at all levels. But if done in a sloppy awkward manner, this step will surely cost you more time than it could ever gain. So it behooves us to practice, and if possible master, the stepped initiation of a racing turn before using it on a course.

The best way to develop this stepped initiation is from straightforward skating on your skis. Everyone has seen this movement and most skiers have done it often enough, especially as a way to avoid walking and poling across flats. First efforts at skating are often rather spaz—galumphing, lurching movements rather than a graceful alternation of push-off from one ski and glide on the other. But it comes quickly. Once you can skate efficiently on your skis—and I assume most readers of this chapter can—all you have to do is progressively spend more time balanced on

FIG. 9.2 SKATING. *The best way to learn the skills essential for the step turns used in racing. Skate with your whole body, letting arms and shoulders move freely with your skating steps.*

the gliding ski, gently easing it into the beginning of a turn before skating off it onto the other ski. That's right, simply prolong the follow-through until you are skating through a series of gentle linked arcs. This is exactly the move you'll use to start your turns in a NASTAR course. At least the longer turns. For quicker changes of direction, you'll just step the top ski straight out to the side. There's no absolute rule. And in gentle slight turns, say across the flats at the bottom of a race course, you may not want to step your skis at all. You'll have to experiment. But remember, an improved racing turn is worthless if you don't turn early enough!

What else can help you take home that NASTAR gold? Practice, for one thing. Larger ski areas often have permanently set-up race courses similar in length and difficulty to NASTAR courses that are automatic, pay-as-you-race operations. You put a dollar in a machine to activate the automatic timing circuit. A good idea.

How about the start of the race? Should you try one of those famous "Killy" starts, leaping up on your poles, kicking your feet and skis up in the air behind you and smashing down through the timing wand at full speed? No way. Unless you're a superb gymnast you'll either fall on your face, or waste the first three turns trying to get your balance and rhythm back.

The same goes for skating vigorously out of the starting gate. Most skiers who try this

FIG. 9.3 STEP TURNS THROUGH A NASTAR COURSE. Basic racing style. The racer starts his turns early, well before the pole, with an effective lateral step. The turn is virtually finished as the racer passes the pole, allowing a steeper, more direct, faster line to the next pole.

lose time and wind up so disorganized that they scramble into their first turn instead of carving smoothly into it. Your best bet is to take several strong poling strokes out of the gate, and then quickly transfer all your attention to an efficient, clean first turn that will set you up for a smooth precise run.

Don't forget our basic idea. You'll do far better concentrating on avoiding mistakes, jerky movements, sideways skidding and the bad, low line that results from late turns than you will by pushing and scrambling for more speed. An efficient precise run is your passport to a NASTAR gold. By now you have all the skills you need, so it's almost in the bag. Good luck!

Racing Resources: Going Beyond "Fun" Racing

I apologize for the title of this section—*all* racing should be fun—but I'm sure you understand what I mean. If you've really gotten a good case of flag fever, if you've decided to take your racing seriously, I'd like to give you a few hints and send you off in the right direction. I'd recommend two steps, one simple and inexpensive, the other requiring major commitment. First, start looking at, and absorbing images of, top-level racing—building up your own inventory of mental motion pictures of the way good racers really ski. And second, sign up for an intensive race camp, so that you can really work out under the guidance of experienced specialized coaches.

The first step involves watching international ski racing on TV, maybe acquiring a couple of video casettes of it; showing up as a spectator at any regional class A, and especially World Cup races, that you can possibly get to; and easiest of all, looking at printed pictures, sequence photos of top racers. One book, *World Cup Ski Technique,* by Olle Larsson and James Major (Park City: Poudre Publishing Co.) stands out as the best of its kind. The photo-montage sequences are exciting, fascinating and informative, and will amply repay your patient study.

The racing-camp option takes more time and commitment but is well worth it. There are a few winter camps, but the majority seem to be scheduled in late spring and early summer. These are usually described and advertised in the final or spring issue of most ski magazines. They last one or two weeks, generally take place on big western mountains like Mammoth or Mt. Hood after the regular ski season has finished, and cost about as much as an average ski vacation. Recently a number of summer race camps have been organized abroad, in the South American Andes and on the well-equipped glacier resorts of the Alps, but the cost is proportionately much greater. A full-on racing camp is the only way I know of for average skiers to have an opportunity to run hundreds and hundreds of gates in one week and receive sophisticated feedback on their performance.

At such race camps, for example, you will

discover that my earlier advice, about always completing your NASTAR turn before passing the pole, is an outrageous simplification of racing strategy. (A simplification amply justified by the average fun racer's tendency to do the exact opposite.) You'll learn about many different "lines" for many different "combinations" of gates. You'll learn faster starts, tactics and strategy. And you'll get faster, day by day. Coaching at these race camps is quite good, and the use of videotaping is common. It will be, I guarantee you, a brand-new sort of skiing experience. So why not try it?

In closing this discussion, I'd like to stress a point of view that has run like a leitmotif throughout this book. Expert skiing is much more than ski racing—it is a multidimensional, multifaceted world of excitement on skis, of which racing is just one part, one aspect. This is so obvious that it wouldn't even bear repeating if the ski industry and ski media hadn't so overdone the racing hype over the years. World Cup racers are indeed the finest skiing athletes of our day—the rewards and the intensity of competition do concentrate an awful lot of talent in this scene. But it's not at all clear to me that top ski racers have any more fun or reap any more personal satisfaction than other expert skiers pursuing their own variations on the skiing experience. I think, now, after a whole book devoted to the *how* of expert skiing, we might profitably take a last look at the more complex and elusive questions of style, motivation and self-expression on skis. The nuances of expert skiing. And we'll do just that in the next chapter.

- *The master strategy for racing: It's less important to struggle for additional speed than to avoid the mistakes that slow you down.*

- *Turn early! Turn early! Turn early! In a NASTAR course try to turn* before, *not after the flag.*

- *Actively stepping to the new outside ski, rather than simply shifting weight to it, is a useful way to adjust your line to clear the pole.*

- *Utilize skating on your skis to develop this "stepped initiation" for racing turns.*

10

POETRY IN MOTION

The Why of Expert Skiing:
Self-Expression on Skis

The path, initially at least,
seems clear: the skier at first

skis dotted lines—turns
traverses, schusses—and finally learns

something called technique; only then
can we discover snow and begin

to carve out real runs from this white
and yielding medium: there isn't any
right

or wrong in such descents
and for a while skiing makes sense.

But with enough time, with no
more fear and a calm mind, the snow

itself begins to change: more and more,
ice resembles powder. As before,

we return to abstractions and find
the mountain has its own lines,

planes, shapes and curves: go back
to skiing dotted lines—a black

on white pattern of movement and form,
pure form—a new world is born.

But we're still not there. Behind
even this intersection of mountain and mind

we sense something always simpler, skiing
not as metaphor but synonym of being.

Skiing has always been a magical sport for me. It is for many people, and I hope for you too. It is also an individual sport par excellence, and hence the magic, joy and excitement that I feel is certainly different from yours. My hope here is that, after an entire book devoted to sharing technique, we can also share some less tangible but equally real insights, the private secrets, the inner dimensions that make skiing a sport like no other.

The title of this chapter, "Poetry in Motion," is neither facetious nor accidental. It seems to me a very good place to begin. There is lots of potential in motion for real poetry—if that motion is free, graceful and rhythmic, strong and powerful, yet light and deft. All of which is a good description of good skiing, of expert skiing, just as it's also a good description of dancing. The parallel between skiing and dancing is one I come back to again and again in my thinking and in my teaching. Both skiing and dancing involve you in a quality of movement that's quite alien to everyday life. When we go to the corner grocery, we walk, we don't soar, float, or whirl through space. And in fact, average dancers don't either. Only the very best, the Fonteyns and Baryshnikovs, great professional artists, attain the lightness and grace that add up to real poetry in motion. The limiting factors are physical gifts and training. It takes unbelievable strength and training to suspend the normal laws of physics and literally soar through space the way the greatest dancers routinely do. Not so in skiing, where the laws of physics, so to speak, are on your side.

This is a simple point that bears repeating. In skiing, the pull of gravity down the slope, and the friction of skis against snow, do ninety percent of the work. These are truly enormous forces, exerting far more energy on moving skiers than the skiers could ever exert with their own muscles. In a strange sense, the skier becomes a superman or superwoman moving through space with an ease never found in everyday life. This is the root of that "state of grace" that even beginners recognize their first day on skis. An excited beginner can fly down those first small practice hills faster than Olympic track-and-field champions could run down them. We shouldn't be able to move like this, we can't, and yet on skis, we do.

What the skier contributes to this dance down the hill then is not force, but timing and coordination—the guiding intelligence and imagination to harness these outside forces and weave them into ecstatic flowing descents. It's a nice image, and an accurate one. And it tends to justify my conviction that all skiers, really, should become experts. Simply because, on skis, they are already liberated from the limits of physical strength that would make such a goal impossible in most other sports. The rest of the picture, the balance and timing, the sequences and patterns of movement, the physical awareness, can be filled in with enough practice and patience. That is all you need to acquire when you learn ski technique, only patterns of movement—not the force or the strength to make such patterns of movement possible. And these patterns are, for the most part, easier to master than double-clutching a stick shift back down into first gear.

The most gifted skiers seem to have arrived on the slopes with such movement patterns built in; ski instructors get no credit for their success. But my goal as a teacher has always involved building up skill patterns where they didn't exist—and I've become convinced that most skiers on the slopes can and should be skiing at a far higher level. All that's missing is the correct sequence of movement patterns to pursue, and the commitment of enough time to accomplish the job. Hence this book.

But the secrets of expert technique, the sequences and patterns I've presented, although truly important, are not in themselves skiing—much less expert skiing. Skiing is what you do with them afterward. The whole reason for studying, practicing or working on technique is to get to the point where you can forget technique altogether. Forget it because it's already there, an acquired part of you, not worth thinking about. It's like learning a foreign language. You have to study French grammar in order to forget it later—but if you don't study it, you'll wind up speaking only pidgin French. And that's the story of most skiers on the slopes. They're doing it but not doing it very well; they're skiing "pidgin." (And now you aren't. Congrats!)

Much interest in ski instruction in recent times has concentrated on the head-trip aspect of skiing—what an expert thinks, or feels, when skiing at a high level. My assumption in this book has been that it's pointless to attempt to think like an expert until legs and body have absorbed the key patterns needed to move like one. But now that we've done just that, the question returns to tempt us: What goes on inside the expert's head? What kind of movie is playing in there? Is there, in fact, an expert's viewpoint on skiing?

My answer is that there's no answer. No one particular way that super-skiers view themselves and their sport. Why bother to learn all this technique, all these advanced skills, if you can't do whatever you want on skis? There's no party line, no right or wrong in real expert skiing, only self-expression. And that's plenty.

This thought opens the door to the subject of style on skis, and at the same time shuts off much pointless debate on what constitutes good style. There are brilliant skiers (mostly racers and coaches) who maintain there is no such thing as style, that true skiing is one hundred percent functional. And there are others (like free-style, ballet competitors) for whom the image a skier projects is all-important. Both are right—but only for themselves—while the majority of skiers fall somewhere in between, and have an intuitive sense of their own style. Style in skiing is more an expression of who you are than of the technique you use. Powerful personalities tend to ski powerfully, graceful spirits ski with grace. Feet together or feet apart, caressing the snow or pounding it into submission, trying to look like a clone of Ingemar Stenmark or happy looking like yourself—who's to judge? And who but you really cares? *De gustibus non disputandum.* I assume that all skiers have their own style. But the expert's style is a more direct personal expression, since skis and body both obey more readily. I repeat: there's no right or wrong in expert skiing.

The way I ski depends entirely on the way I feel on any particular day. Having mastered the easiest way to link two turns, for example, via dynamic anticipation, there's no absolute reason you have to do it that way. Most of the time you probably will, because it's efficient and because your mind is elsewhere—creating great runs rather than perfect turns. In general, individual moves, individual turns and small groups of turns are what ski technique is all about. Going beyond technique means thinking (and living) in bigger terms—whole runs; long and continuous adventures on skis that can take you from mountaintops to valley floors, from one life zone to another, from midwinter to early spring in the course of a single flying descent. Some mornings you'll be consumed with a visceral need for excitement, other days you may feel detached, calm and serene. As a real expert, you'll find yourself crafting runs that interpret the mountain according to your whim, your mood.

One hallmark of great skiing, though, is the way experts always seem to adjust their skiing to the mountain in front of them, responding intuitively to the new shapes and conditions they encounter—the dips and rolls and fallaways, the twists and surprises. Perhaps confidence in one's own technique liberates the spirit to look around and see what's really there. By contrast, the inexperienced skier often seems locked into a one-dimensional survival style—the best he or she can do—in which one trusty, dependable turn is repeated doggedly down each and every slope. Such skiers seem oblivious to the invitations and temptations of the terrain in front of them, never skiing the "big shapes," never discovering how different one run, one mountain, one day on skis can be from another. Nor does one always have to ski *with* the mountain—launching big swoopers over God's own moguls, the natural megarolls in the terrain; stretching turns out on the flats or tightening them up on the steep; following the not always natural curves of bumps. Skiing at cross-purposes to the terrain can be an exciting challenge too;

and it's a giggle (expert skiing is *not* deadly serious). It's also another real response to the mountain in front of you.

So I guess I ought to modify my earlier answer. The point of expert skiing isn't just self-expression. Exploring and interpreting the mountain, exploring and reinventing the skiing experience are a daily part of it too. And if that sounds open-ended, it is. Skiing certainly is. Ten years from now we'll all be skiing differently. The snowy dance never stops. I hope this book has been equally open-ended for you —an initiation into expert skiing but not the definitive wrap-up of it.

What else can I add? Perhaps only that skiing is such an intense experience that there are times when you can hardly bear it by yourself. Individual sport par excellence it may be, but for me the best moments on skis are those I spend skiing with my friends. I have to say, if expert sking is a magical sport, sharing it with someone you love doubles the magic. Breakthroughs can be shared too; be sure to share yours. You'll have as much pleasure doing so as I've had writing this book.

AFTERWORD

Gear for Expert Skiing

If there's one idea that's dominated this whole book, it's surely that in expert skiing, more and more of the "work" is done by the equipment. The skier's brute force is replaced by the subtle and cunning interaction of well-designed skis with snow. It's a good idea and it works. But what about this equipment?

I've already permitted myself a few generalizations about modern skis, telling you, for example, that they are typically softer in flex and at the same time torsionally more rigid than earlier generations of skis, which allows them to carve as never before. But are all skis created equal? Will any pair of boots do? Must skiers become expert ski mechanics to be sure they're getting all the performance they paid for out of their sleek new gear? Whom can you trust when it comes to selecting equipment? And what do you look for? How can you tell when your skis need tuning, waxing, replacing? Good questions, all of which I'll try to answer—along with a few others—in this last section.

I'll start by confirming your worst suspicions: Yes, equipment is terribly important, so important that often skiers' mediocre performances can be blamed directly on their gear. And what's worse, most average, even dedicated skiers are skiing on equipment so bad that it seems to me a miracle that they can turn at all. Well, that's not quite accurate. I really shouldn't say *on such bad equipment* but rather *on equipment in such bad shape.* More than once in the last few years I've swapped skis for a run or two with students who wore the same size boots I did—and found to my surprise that I couldn't turn. At least not easily, not without a struggle, not the way I wanted to. And I'm not talking about old hand-me-down skis, but the latest highly touted models, which had cost a pretty penny but had never been properly prepared for skiing. So equipment really is critical.

We'll look at the equipment needs of expert (and would-be expert) skiers item by item, saving the most important topic—ski preparation and tuning—for last.

Boots: Beyond Simple Comfort

Consider modern boots: skiers' winged heels, or molded plastic torture devices? Mostly I incline to the former view—uncomfortable boots are, fortunately, becoming rarer and rarer. Comfort has always been a major issue in ski boots, simply because many of our balance reflexes are associated with pressure sensitivity in the soles of the feet—and if your boots hurt, then your balance goes all to hell. But comfort isn't everything.

For a number of years, too many manufacturers traded performance for ease of fit by pushing comfy but low-performance rear-entry boots for most skiers. Only Salomon seemed able to make a high-performance rear-entry boot. Eventually the boot industry gave up and went back to more conventional multiple-buckle, front-entry boots with some of the fit/comfort features of the rear-entry models thrown in. It's a pretty happy compromise. So-called mid-entry boots provide the anatomical support of traditional designs, but because the upper shaft tilts back, the skier's foot can slip in with less (or no) grunting, scraping, and cursing. Your ideal boot feels like a cross between velvet and iron—soft enough to feel good, stiff enough to give solid support all around the foot, on both sides of the ankle and gently, evenly against your shin.

Boot needs, in fact, vary far more between individual skiers than is the case with skis. There is perhaps no such thing as a normal foot, much less a normal "perfect" leg. But reasonable ankle flex is at the top of my shopping list for boots. Beware of boots that fight back when you flex forward. If you feel as though you've hit a sudden wall, the boot is too stiff. It should give in forward flex, progressively resisting more and more as your knees flex further forward. If the front shaft of your leg feels trapped and immobile in a pair of boots, if you can't flex them just standing on the shop floor, don't even bother to take them out on the hill. They won't work.

Some companies make ideal boots for narrow feet, and some quite the opposite, so I can't tell you in advance what brand or model will be right for your feet. I can, however, warn you about the top-of-the-line, just-like-the-World-Cup-racers syndrome—the tendency to walk into a ski shop and ask for the latest racing model. Smaller skiers, petite women, and those with short rather than long legs should avoid any boots labeled "racing model." These boots will be far too stiff for such skiers. All boots today provide adequate lateral support, so don't fall into the trap of thinking that only racing gear will deliver high performance. Many instructors do just that, partly because they want to look cool, like the big boys. Far better are boots that are custom-tailored to your needs and your feet.

Customizing one's ski boots is no longer an idle fancy but an everyday reality since many models now have built-in canting, as well as forward-lean and forward-flex adjustments. Canting, of course, is the lateral adjustment of the boot's upper shaft (and sometimes the sole) to conform to, or compensate for, some unusual curvature or slant of the leg. For some skiers this makes all the difference in their ability to stand on the edge of their foot and thus control the edge of their ski. But you shouldn't depend blindly on ski shop personnel to adjust the boots' canting for you. These adjustments are mostly very simple and you can play with them yourself until you feel you've achieved the best edging and the most comfortable stance on your skis. Trust your own instincts. I say this because there must be at least a half dozen different approaches to canting boots. Different ski shops will follow a different theory of how to cant the boot shafts without stopping to figure out precisely what you might need—and without knowing how you ski. In some larger resorts, however, there are now a few specialized shops that do nothing but customize ski boot fit—and these are well worth a visit.

Some shops can also cast custom footbeds to be placed inside the boot for a better fit and more control. At least that's the theory. Once again, not all custom footbeds work for all feet, so the final test is whether they improve your skiing and your "ski feel." If they don't, pitch them. You will only have lost $35 to $50 but learned a good lesson—namely, that no one understands your own feet the way you do. I fuss around a lot until my boots are just right, and I recommend you do too. Remember the very first point I made in chapter one: More than anything else, *we ski with our feet.*

Modern Bindings: A Safety Net That Works

Binding manufacturers deserve a vote of thanks. They've made incredible strides over the years. And recently, thanks to improved bindings, ski injury statistics have begun to fall dramatically after years and years of relatively modest improvement. But these manufacturers are businessmen as well as technological wizards, and in their desire to sell as many bindings as possible, they have done something I disapprove of. Instead of producing only the very best binding they are capable of designing and manufacturing, every company produces a full range of ski bindings for every "price point" in the market. Some are cheap, some expensive, most in between; and believe me, the variations in performance are as great as the spread in price.

You already know what I'm about to say. Buy only the most expensive, so-called top-of-the-line bindings any company has to offer! (But again, not the racing models, please, which are generally nothing more than top models with extra-heavy springs and unrealistically high release settings.) The extra money top-of-the-line bindings cost will be well worth it. The top models are generally more elastic, which means that they will begin to release under a severe load or twist and then come back to center if the force is not sustained. This helps the binding distinguish between the momentary forces and impacts typical of high-level skiing (hitting the lip of a big bump sideways, for example) and the more sustained forces that could cause injury. It's a critical factor. The ski-industry assumptions have been that not all skiers need highly elastic bindings—and also that beginners and casual skiers won't pay the extra dollar for these mechanically more sophisticated binding systems. I strongly disagree. The more elastic the binding, the lower a release setting you can use and still keep your skis on your feet. This is important since unwanted releases can also cause injuries. And that seems to me a plus for any level skier. The sort of skier I've written this book for, however, really has no choice. Top-of-the-line bindings are basic equipment for expert skiers, period—money well spent.

More and more, the best bindings offer an upward release function at the toe. There is a lot of evidence that this function helps to reduce or eliminate certain knee injuries. And I should tell you that injuries to knee ligaments (like the dreaded ACL, or anterior cruciate ligament) seem to be particularly common today. Perhaps we just notice them more because the conventional injuries—breaks and sprains—have diminished in number. So if bindings with upward release at the toe can help stack the odds in your favor, why not use them?

You should also own a set of runaway straps to be used only on real deep powder days. Ski brakes have long since replaced straps for everyday skiing, and with good reason. I have a couple of scars from the bad old days when my windmilling skis, held to my feet by straps, swung around and caught me in the side and the chin. However, if your ski releases in deep snow, it can't windmill around and hit you—the resistance of the powder around it is too great—and if it isn't attached, you can literally spend hours looking for it beneath the snow. You might not find it till spring. I consider some kind of clip-on straps a must for deep snow.

Poles: Neglected Step-children of the Equipment Scene

Often we see ambitious skiers shell out small fortunes for new gear—skis, boots, bindings, the works—yet continue skiing with ten- or fifteen-year-old poles as though they didn't matter. Wrong! In some situations—in bumps, for example, where the deft lightning-fast use of your poles is essential—heavy, clunky old poles can defeat you as totally as stiff skis, uncomfortable boots, or a negative attitude. Ski poles are precision tools, not clubs. And although there are dozens and dozens of different models and brands of ski poles sold everywhere—in dozens of different designer colors—there are perhaps only a total of a half dozen that are adequate for expert skiing. By adequate, I mean sufficiently light and well balanced. A good pole almost plants itself, in the right spot at the right time. Think I'm kidding? You'll see.

Look for adjustable straps—and snug them up so your fingers don't have to grip the pole as tightly. I prefer poles whose grips are tilted slightly forward. This has the effect of extending your poles toward the new turn even faster—a big plus in moguls. The big news in pole design these last few years has been the introduction of composite Fiberglas shafts, which are rapidly replacing light aluminum.

They look new and sexy; some are pencil thin. But many composite poles are terribly balanced. Light weight, it turns out, is no substitute for well-balanced distribution of weight along the shaft of the pole, since all that really counts is how the pole feels in your hands, in use. The points I want to make are that expert skiers pay quite a lot of attention to their poles—and that pole choice is both subjective and important. Lightness, balance, and quickness—these are positive qualities in skiing itself, and no less so in ski poles.

Skis: The Critical Interface

In your quest to become an expert skier, you've quickly realized that your skis are much more than accessories, or even tools; they are your allies and partners, companions through amazing adventures. Ironically, I would say that it's not so important to have great skis in order to break through into expert skiing—as long as you don't have lousy ones, and as long as they're reasonably tuned. However, once you've become a dyed-in-the-wool expert, you will probably become very particular indeed about your skis.

There was a period not so long ago when short skis were all the vogue. Many intermediates are still cruising around on relics from this era, with the idea—also a legacy of the same period—that long or "full length" skis are somehow hard to turn. It just ain't so anymore—although somewhat shorter than normal skis ("learning length" skis, between shoulder and head high) are still a good idea for first-time beginners and novices.

But serious skiers belong on serious skis. And the variety of good skis available nowadays is greater than ever. The only real danger is winding up with skis that are too stiff. Although modern skis, by and large, are not stiff—and statistically skis have been getting softer and softer for years—you still have to watch out for "racing" models. Calling a ski a racing ski is sometimes just a PR gimmick to sell more skis to gung-ho skiers. But some companies market real, thoroughbred, no-nonsense racing skis. And for many skiers these spell trouble. We've already learned that if any part of the ski is going to break loose and skid, it will be the tail, and this is doubly true at higher racing speeds. So true racing models tend to have an unbalanced flex pattern, with the tail and rear of the ski much stiffer than the front. This is helpful for "holding" at high speeds on very hard surfaces, but it is a real pain in soft snow, in bumps, and at slower or medium speeds. Sure, all ski designs are a compromise. But I like and tend to recommend the sort of compromises that cover the widest spectrum. One happy compromise is the so-called bump ski offered by many ski manufacturers. It is a racing ski with a softened tip and tail for better absorption in rough terrain and a smoother, more forgiving ride. Another new compromise is the soft GS ski. Giant Slalom skis used to be bears to turn in tight spots, making them suitable only for big turns and high-speed cruising. But in recent years GS models with much more sidecut than ever before have appeared; and they are now competing with soft slalom skis as all-around pleasure skis. Just beware of the most extreme, specialized racing machines. In my experience, relatively soft and even flexing skis do a lot more things well. The remarkable torsional rigidity of all modern skis guarantees that even quite soft skis will still grip well and carve precise arcs.

But which modern skis? I want to suggest a foolproof strategy for choosing new skis—new skis that will do wonders for your skiing. It's simple. Always, *always,* try out demo pairs of the skis you're interested in first, making sure you rent demos from a ski shop that keeps its demos perfectly tuned and waxed. If you can't tell any difference in the way you're skiing, then don't buy them. If you're amazed at how much better you ski on the demos, then you've found a winner, and you can write a big check for them with a light heart. (But think twice before rushing out to buy a pair of specialized fat powder skis of the kind I talked about in chapter seven. They're great, but you can probably rent them for powder days, which, alas, occur all too infrequently.)

Personally, I reckon that a pair of skis that will improve my skiing is worth almost anything, and that's precisely what I look for when I try out new skis, not just another pair that skis as well as my current set. Believe me, there are skis that will open up new perspectives for you by responding to your technique with more precision, more liveliness, more subtlety. You have to discover these skis by word of mouth and by trying them personally. You certainly can't glean much from the annual ski reports published in the ski press because these magazines can't afford to alienate their advertisers by panning poor skis. And don't be taken in when a salesman says, "These are really great skis, but of course they take a while to get used to." One run is enough for you to know if you've got a magic pair of skis on your feet—or dogs. Yet even the absolute all-time best pair of skis is next to worthless if it isn't well tuned.

Skis Fit to Ski On: Tuning for Expert Skiing

Nowadays most skiers are far more conscious of ski preparation and ski tuning than they were five and ten years back—but still not conscious enough. A mediocre pair of well-tuned skis will far outperform a fantastic pair of skis in bad shape. So just what do I mean when I say "well tuned"?

A well-tuned ski has a running surface that is smooth rather than scratched, flat rather than hollow or concave, and its edges are smooth to the touch, with no burrs, nicks, or jagged spots on them. And that's just the beginning, the minimum. Whether the edges need be "sharp" or not, or only partially sharp, really depends on the snow conditions. For example, ice demands super-sharp edges; on packed powder, you really don't need sharp edges at all; and often in "soapy," grabby, spring snow conditions, you have to dull your edges with ultra-fine 400 grit sandpaper to keep them from catching.

Many modern skis perform best with so-called beveled edges—that is, when the ski bottoms are not completely flat all the way out to the edge but are "taken down" in the last few centimeters to meet the edge at slightly more than a right angle (see fig. on p. 286).

And, finally, your skis should have fast, well-waxed bases. This is necessary in order to ski well, not merely to go fast. Of course, a correctly waxed ski is fast, but it's also slippery—and reduced friction between ski base and snow means that in many instances you can control the ski with less muscular force. Strangely, you can ski a waxed pair of skis much more effortlessly at extremely slow speeds than an unwaxed pair just because of this slippery quality.

You're convinced, I'm sure. But how do you go about keeping your skis in good shape? How much do you have to learn and do yourself? How much can you trust a ski shop to do for you? You can certainly learn to do it all. It's not too demanding and can even be fun, sort of. But you'll need a work bench of some sort. And look every year in various ski magazines for detailed illustrated articles on how to tune your skis; you'll find these are a pretty good source of information.

You can also ask one of the ski mechanics

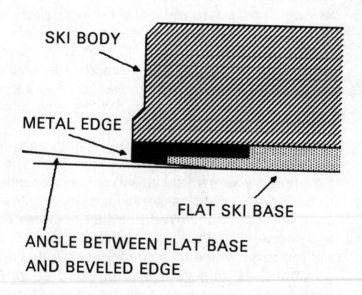

SKI BODY

METAL EDGE

FLAT SKI BASE

**ANGLE BETWEEN FLAT BASE
AND BEVELED EDGE**

This close-up cross-section drawing shows what is meant by a beveled ski bottom. The edge of the base has been filed down more than normal so that it no longer meets the sidewall of the ski at a right angle. Beveled tuning can enhance the performance of most modern skis. The degree or amount of bevel shown in this drawing is exaggerated for clarity; it is actually a very small and subtle angle.

at a local shop to show you the whole drill. These guys are the unsung heroes of skiing, and they're usually glad to share their experience with anyone curious enough to ask. In some ways, ski tuning now is harder than it used to be, because most modern skis really do perform better with beveled edges, and beveling the bases with a file is a fine and delicate art, since we're talking about an angle only one or two degrees off the horizontal. Fortunately, there are a number of special beveling tools, and I would really recommend that you buy one if you want the full, hands-on, ski-tuning experience.

But you don't have to master the art of ski tuning to ski on perfect skis any more than you have to be a master mechanic to drive a Porsche. It's sufficient to know when to take the Porsche, or the skis, in for a tune up—and to have enough knowledge to cope with roadside, or trailside, problems. At a minimum, you'll want to get three things and learn to use them: a true bar, a small sharpening stone, and a piece of 400 grit wet/dry sandpaper.

A *true bar* is a small, perfectly machined bar or cylinder of hard steel that you can lay on the bases of your skis and slide along to check whether they are flat or concave. Telltale light under the bar near the center of the base is a sure sign that your skis need work. And it's very common. You see, the action of skiing tends to wear down the plastic material in the center of the base more than at the edges, producing a hollow or concave base. This is especially true on granular spring snow, but happens—though less quickly—on winter powder too. This results in edges that are "higher" than the base. They dig too deeply into the snow and hang up, and you start turning with brute force again. Skiers often speak of "railed" bases. But whatever you call them, they're bad news. Hollowed, concave bases need major surgery. The only effective solution is to take them to a ski shop that has state-of-the-art stone grinding machines.

However, simply stone grinding the bases flat is only a beginning. The ski bases then need a fine finish. This used to be possible only with careful hand filing, but now another generation of base-prepping machines can produce a microscopic structure in the plastic base material for greater speed and more efficient waxing. These machines can also mill a differential bevel along the ski's bottom, beveling the tip and tail a couple of degrees, an angle that tapers progressively to zero, or a perfectly flat ski just underfoot. This is a nice refinement that seems to work well with many of the latest skis.

Try to discover the very best ski-tuning shop in the area where you ski; there is always a *best* ski tuner. The way to do this is to ask hot local skiers and instructors where they get their own skis worked on. Ski shops at major ski areas simply have more experience with ski tuning than any city shops; after all, they do more pairs of skis and get more feedback about their ski tuning.

A pocket *sharpening stone* is a tiny and cunning object that is worth its weight in gold early in the season, when eager-beaver skiers are often sliding on a surface of mixed snow and rock. Rocks gouge the P-Tex bases of your skis, and they nick and burr the edges of your skis. Gouges have to be filled in with melted P-Tex, and scrapped flat, either at home or by a shop. But the burrs and jagged spots along the edge—which interfere terribly with the smooth sliding and arcing of the ski—can be taken care of on the slope or, more likely, at lunch. Pull out your trusty stone and rub it along both planes of the edge, bottom and side. That's all you need to do. The edge will once again feel smooth to the touch, and your skis will behave normally. Why not use a file? Hitting a rock actually case-hardens a thin layer of steel along the edge to such a degree that files no longer cut. Only a sharpening stone works. You can get a tiny Carborundum stone at the hardware store for a couple of bucks, and keep it in your parka pocket during periods when the snow cover is less than perfect.

The final item, *super-fine sandpaper,* is used to dull back the tip and tail sections of the edge as needed for very "grabby" snow conditions. A "sharp" edge, by the way, is nothing more than a perfect, clean angle between bottom and side, not a knife blade. To dull the edge, run the ultra-fine sandpaper gently along it, taking care not to rub too hard or really try to round the edge off. We're talking subtleties here, but you'll feel a big difference. Scraped, wettish spring snow is very grabby, and you'll certainly know when your tips start hooking, or when your tails catch and refuse to turn. Dull the edges from the tips and tails progressively back toward the bindings, a little at a time, until the skis stop grabbing.

I would say that this is about the minimum ski-tuning knowledge you can get away with: the goal of expert skiing is simply unobtainable unless your skis are in good shape. The reason I suggest that everyone buy a true bar—even though most skiers have never even heard of one—is that as your skis get progressively more out of tune, you will unconsciously adjust your skiing to them. And it will completely go to pot without you even being aware that you're working far too hard. It's that gradual. If you can deal with the problem as soon as your ski bases begin to get hollow by checking with your true bar, you'll be way ahead of the crowd.

About waxing: ideally, you should wax your skis or have them waxed every day. I know it's very hard for many skiers to do this, but try. If you're a weekend skier, maybe you can get away with waxing once for the whole weekend. But really, it's such a joy to ski on fast-waxed skis that you should simply get into the habit of waxing as often as possible. Waxing means hot-waxing: melting the right wax onto and into the ski bases with an iron, then scraping it down to a very thin layer. It can be a messy job, so don't wax in the living room of your best friend's ski condo.

You may be thinking by now that this Lito sounds like a real fanatic with his true bars and 400-grit sandpaper and waxing the skis every day—but, of course, he's a professional skier, I'm not. Close, but not exact. You are, after all, an expert skier by now, so you really *can* tell the difference. Perfectly prepared skis are your passport to another world. Don't let this passport expire!

Lito Tejada-Flores

BREAKTHROUGH ON SKIS

Lito Tejada-Flores has lived a lifelong love
affair with mountains and mountain
sports—rockclimbing, mountaineering,
whitewater kayaking, and, above all,
skiing. He has made first ascents from
the Alps to Patagonia and skied on five
continents. But his greatest pleasure has
been to share these passions with others.

As ski instructor and trainer of ski
instructors at Squaw Valley, Bear Valley,
Telluride, and Vail; as author of three
earlier books on backcountry skiing and
kayaking; as technical editor of *Powder*
magazine and contributing editor of
Skiing magazine, Tejada-Flores has
translated experience into insight and
insight into progress for thousands of
fellow enthusiasts. *Breakthrough on Skis*
is the result of more than twenty years
of ski teaching and of his conviction that

there really is an expert inside almost every skier.

He has recently completed a video tape, *Breakthrough on Skis: The Video,* a visual journey through the same steps to expert skiing presented in this book.

Lito Tejada-Flores lives at 9,000 feet in Telluride, Colorado, with photographer Linde Waidhofer, with whom he founded Western Eye Press. Together they have created and published a number of photo books on the Rocky Mountain West, a series of skiers' guidebooks, books on the history and environment of the western states, and this year moved into the video arena with *Breakthrough on Skis: The Video.*